*There are some things
in [Paul's letters] hard to
understand, which the
ignorant and unstable
twist to their own
destruction, as they do the
other scriptures. You
therefore, beloved,
knowing this beforehand,
beware lest you be carried
away with the error of
lawless men and lose
your own stability.
2 Peter 3:16-17*

*In religion,
What damned error,
but some sober brow
Will bless and approve
it with a text,
Hiding the grossness
with fair ornament?
Shakespeare,* The
Merchant of Venice

SCRIPTURE TWISTING

20 Ways the Cults Misread the Bible

JAMES W. SIRE

InterVarsity Press
Downers Grove
Illinois 60515

InterVarsity Press is the book-publishing division of Inter-Varsity Christian Fellowship, a student movement active on campus at hundreds of universities, colleges and schools of nursing. For information about local and regional activities, write IVCF, 233 Langdon St., Madison, WI 53703.

Distributed in Canada through InterVarsity Press, 1875 Leslie St., Unit 10, Don Mills, Ontario M3B 2M5, Canada.

Biblical quotations, unless otherwise noted, are from the Revised Standard Version of the Bible, copyrighted 1946, 1952, © 1971, 1973, and are used by permission.

ISBN 0-87784-611-1

Printed in the United States of America

Library of Congress Cataloging in Publication Data
Sire, James W
    Scripture twisting.

    Includes bibliographical references and indexes.
    1. Bible–Hermeneutics.   2. Bible–Evidences,
authority, etc.   3. Cults.   I. Title.
BS476.S58   220.6'01   80-19309
ISBN 0-87784-611-1

| 17 | 16 | 15 | 14 | 13 | 12 | 11 | 10 | 9 | 8 | 7 | 6 | 5 | 4 | 3 | 2 |
| 94 | 93 | 92 | 91 | 90 | 89 | 88 | 87 | 86 | 85 | 84 | 83 | 82 | 81 | | |

Preface

I wish I had been there. It would have made a good opening for the preface of this book. There he was—Swami Satchitananda, head of the Integral Yoga Institute, addressing a capacity crowd at the Masonic Auditorium in San Francisco.[1] " 'Blessed are the pure in heart,' Jesus said, 'for they shall see God,' " quoted the swami. And moments later, he explained these words something like this: "Yes, blessed are those who purify their consciousness, for they shall see themselves as God."

It is just such a perversion of Jesus' teaching that this book is all about. How do so many different gurus and religious groups find it so easy to appropriate the Bible to their own use? How can the swami turn a profound beatitude into a blasphemous equation of God and fallen man?

And, well we might ask, for the swami is not alone. The

Mormon missionary begins with James 1:5 ("If any of you lack wisdom, let him ask of God" KJV) and soon is teaching that both God the Father and Jesus the Son have glorified physical bodies. Mary Baker Eddy says the opening line of the Lord's Prayer means, "Our Father-Mother God, all-harmonious." The Jehovah's Witnesses refer to John 1:1 ("the Word was with God, and the Word was God") and explain how this teaches that Jesus is neither coequal nor coeternal with the Father.

As Christians and, we trust, good readers of the Bible, we need all the help we can get to be sure we are reading the Scripture accurately, that we are indeed worshiping the one true God. That's why I wrote this book: to help all of us—myself as much as anyone—to become better readers of the Scriptures, more devoted followers of our Lord Jesus Christ, more effective communicators of God's truth to all people. But the book also seeks a special audience—those being led, as are so many today, by false teachers into false doctrines and perhaps eventually into eternal darkness. May God use this book to help stem the tide of error.

Chapter 1
The Methodology of Misreading: An Introduction

T his book has its origin in an odd sensation in the pit of my stomach. Now, I like to think of myself as cool and rational. Show me a great work of art and, rather than melting before its rays of beauty, I will probably begin to analyze it. That's what makes this particular book so exceptional for me. It started from a feeling—a physical sensation, and not a pleasant one either.

Attack on the Bible
The situation was this. To give me some needed background before editing a book on what happens at death, I was reading *Afterlife: Reports from the Threshold of Death,* a book by Archie Matson, a liberal Protestant minister.[1] Matson's book is filled with stories of people who claim to have died and come back to life, stories of mediums who receive

messages from the Other Side, stories of ghosts and adventure tales of those who say their "souls" have left their bodies and have traveled to the mysterious Waiting World that lurks at the edge of consciousness and is only fully penetrated at death.

But none of this spiritism moved me. Actually, I had read all this before, and it doesn't take long for such stories to become banal and boring. What struck me was the author's attitude, which surfaced again and again, that the Bible, if rightly understood, does two things. First, it supports the occult interpretation of life—the occult world view. Second, the Bible is not to be trusted as a guide because it is not always correct in its view of life, especially of life beyond the grave. In other words, Matson seemed to be using the Scripture where it served his purposes and rejecting it or ignoring it when it did not.

As a Christian the Bible means a lot to me. It has been my companion for years. I have learned that its words are God's Word, its commands his will, its perspective on life the only true one. Of course, it has puzzled me with its enigmas and the depth of its insight. I am often frustrated by what I believe God is demanding of me through the words on its pages. It encourages me, but it breaks me. It thrills me and it frightens me.

But one thing it does not do: it does not come to me in such a way that I can pick and choose what to hold as true or false. As a Christian I find myself under its authority. And that is why reading Matson gave me such a sinking feeling. For Matson, with what seemed to me incredible ease, placed himself, modern science and even mediumship above God's Word.

The real blow to my solar plexus, however, came late in his book, when I began to read chapter eleven, "The Bible —Shackle or Spur?" Here's how the chapter begins:

The Bible itself and its various interpretations which

have become a part of traditional theology form the biggest obstacle to the study and understanding of life beyond death by the average man.... There are two strains of teaching and belief in the Bible which have largely shackled progress in all forms of psychic research among Christian people in the past. One of these is the repeated condemnation of communication with the dead in the Old Testament as illustrated by the story of King Saul and the woman of Endor.... The other scriptural idea blocking our pursuit of this path is the belief that the so-called New Testament theology of resurrection and future judgement invalidate anything research may claim to discover. It is possible that the opposite is true; that is, that the results of careful investigation may force a rewriting of some of our theology.[2]

This direct attack on the authority of Scripture in matters about which it speaks clearly struck me hard. Then worse followed as Matson began to twist biblical texts out of shape either to show how they supported his occult world view or how they contradicted other biblical texts. His caricature of traditional biblical interpretation infuriated me: "The idea that every word is literally true is so obviously false that we need not belabor the matter."[3] This is, of course, a cheap shot at the sophisticated attempt of traditional biblical scholars to get at the original meaning of the texts.

A Methodology of Misreading
As I read Matson further, I began to see that he had what could not unfairly be called a methodology of misreading. As I studied this chapter closely, I began to list the various ways he misunderstood Scripture and argued from his misunderstanding. Matson set up straw men (like the literal view of interpreting Scripture), used innuendo, argued in a circle, failed to take into account other relevant biblical

texts, engaged in name-calling, misrepresented the biblical data, charged contradictions in the Bible that are clearly not there, and drew wild, speculative conclusions. In spite of evidence to the contrary, for example, Matson concludes at one point that it is "fairly certain that the early Christians felt they were free to make whatever contact they could with the dead, and that they had the example of their Master and disciples in so doing."[4]

This study set me to thinking. How do people in various religious movements, especially those involved with the occult or the cults, interpret Scripture? Many cults claim to have a high regard for it. Jehovah's Witnesses, for example, claim the Bible as their sole authority.[5] The Mormons place it first in their list of Scriptures.[6] The Unification Church of Sun Myung Moon also gives it an authoritative position, as does Mary Baker Eddy and Christian Science.[7] Even the Maharishi Mahesh Yogi, founder of Transcendental Meditation, and other writers in the Eastern traditions quote favorably from the Bible.[8] If traditional Christianity affirms the Bible as its sole authority—*sola Scriptura,* as the Reformers said—how can these very different religious movements claim Scripture for their own?

The obvious answer is the right one, I believe. They can only do so by violating the principles of sound literary interpretation. Quite frankly, what I hope this book will show is that the extent to which heretical doctrines are said to be based on Scripture is the extent to which misreading has taken place. Of course, not all doctrines held by traditional Christians have an equally firm biblical base. There is room for disagreement, for example, between Christians who hold that baptism is for adult believers only and those who argue that, like circumcision, baptism is also for the children of believers. The case for either view is problematic, and serious Christians have drawn different conclusions. But both groups believe baptism is an impor-

·tant rite; the disagreement is on a lesser point. And neither group is likely to feel baptism for the dead (a rite practiced by Mormons) is to be practiced though there is one (and only one) allusion to it in the Bible (1 Cor. 15:29).

There are difficulties in Scripture—passages which are obscure, references which are unclear, doctrines which to equally serious and committed Christians seem problematic. This we must admit. In fact, it is often in just these difficult areas that cult teaching makes its entry. Obscurities, like baptism for the dead, become key doctrines or important practices.

The point is that for the central core of the Christian faith—what C. S. Lewis calls "mere" Christianity—the biblical evidence is overwhelming. The deity of Christ, the triune nature of God, the creation of the world by God, the sinfulness of all humanity, salvation by God's grace through faith, the resurrection of the dead—these and many other such matters are clearly taught in Scripture. Yet all of these have been challenged by one cult or another, and sometimes these challenges have been based—so the cult may claim—on the Bible itself.

The Purpose of the Book
It is just this, therefore, that I want to address in this book: How do religious groups that significantly diverge from orthodox Christianity use the Scripture? What can we learn from this misuse about our own reading of the Bible? How can we put an understanding of this misuse to work for us in responding to cult evangelists and to friends caught up in various spiritual counterfeits? How can we keep from going astray ourselves? After all, Sun Myung Moon was once a Presbyterian and Edgar Cayce once taught Sunday school.

Put in a positive way, the purpose of this book is to provide a guide to the methodology of misunderstanding that characterizes cultic use of Scripture. Primarily it provides a catalog of reading errors—not a list of all the false doctrines drawn from misreading but a list of the errors made in the process of interpreting the Scripture. I have been able to isolate twenty separate kinds of mistakes—from simple misquotation of Scripture to complex, deliberate retranslation of the text to fit a preconceived idea; from ignoring the immediate context of a passage of Scripture to mistaking a literal reference for a figurative one or vice versa. (All twenty are summarized in appendix one.)

It is important, too, to realize what this book does not attempt to do. It is *not* a guide to the cults themselves. This would be a topic on its own—and a huge one. Second, this book is not a list of each false idea people claim to find in Scripture. That, too, would be a giant project, for everything from the notion that God has a body to the idea that Ezekiel saw a space ship "way up in the middle of the air" would have to be listed. Third, this book is not even a handbook to how each cult uses the Bible. Of course, many of these uses will be mentioned in illustration, but no attempt is made here to distinguish between the ways the Bible is used by the Mormons as contrasted with the Jehovah's Witnesses.

What is attempted is, I believe, more helpful than all of these. For, if a Christian knows how the Bible is or can be misread, he or she can be properly wary of any evangelist's claim that the Bible teaches any bizarre doctrine at all. With new cults springing up almost daily, what is needed is a general defense against all perversions of God's Word.

A knowledge of misreading goes well with developing good reading habits. Christians who respect biblical authority have a special burden to read right. We, too, are prone to fall into error. In fact, none of us is absolutely right about what God's Word really means. That is why we must ourselves return daily to the Bible—reading and rereading, thinking and rethinking, obeying what we grasp, correcting our earlier readings as new insight is given us, constantly crosschecking our grasp of Scripture with our pastor, our fellow Christians and with the historic understanding of Scripture by orthodox Christianity.

We should, as well, secure at least a small library of biblical scholarship: a Bible dictionary such as the *New Bible Dictionary* (Eerdmans), a one-volume Bible commentary such as the *New Bible Commentary* (Eerdmans), a Bible concordance such as Cruden's or Strong's or Young's. Beyond these there are many excellent commentary series such as the Tyndale New Testament Commentaries (Eerdmans) or the Tyndale Old Testament Commentaries (IVP). All of these books are written by Christian scholars who employ the principles of good reading and deal carefully with Scripture. And, while the various commentators may disagree on technical details of interpretation, all are committed to viewing the Scripture as authoritative in all areas of Christian life and thought.

The Authority of Scripture

All readers bring to their reading presuppositions which govern the way they will finally interpret what they read. That is why each of us as Christians needs to be clear about our attitude toward Scripture. I want to state at the outset my own position. If you as a reader wish to take another view, that is, of course, your privilege. You should know, however, what mine is so that you can place this book in its intended frame of reference.

Two formal statements about the Bible, framed by others, I find helpful. The first, a brief one, is found in the doctrinal basis of Inter-Varsity Christian Fellowship, which holds to "the unique Divine inspiration, entire trustworthiness and authority of the Bible." In a nutshell this affirms, as do I, that the Bible originates with God. He has inspired (breathed into it) his truth, though not by a mechanical dictation such that the personality and mentality of the human authors of the Bible has been by-passed. That would contradict the obvious human character of Scripture. Rather, *"in many and various ways* God spoke of old to our fathers *by the prophets"* (Heb. 1:1). But, though the ways were "many and various," it is God who spoke. That is why the Bible is entirely trustworthy and authoritative, as the IVCF statement concludes.

Moreover, no further claim to revelation is allowed. The Bible is "unique" in its expression of God's truth. This sets aside the Mormon community of authority which includes the Bible but adds the Book of Mormon, *Doctrine and Covenants* and the *Pearl of Great Price.*

A second formal statement, somewhat more elaborate, was developed as Article 2 of the Lausanne Covenant (1974):

We affirm the divine inspiration, truthfulness and authority of both Old and New Testament Scriptures in their entirety as the only written Word of God, without error in all that it affirms, and the only infallible rule of faith and practice. We also affirm the power of God's Word to accomplish his purpose of salvation. The message of the Bible is addressed to all mankind. For God's revelation in Christ and in Scripture is unchangeable. Through it the Holy Spirit still speaks today. He illumines the minds of God's people in every culture to preserve its truth freshly through their own eyes and thus discloses to the whole church ever more of the many-colored wisdom of God. (2 Tim. 3:16; 2 Pet. 1:21; John 10:35; Isa. 55:11; 1 Cor. 1:21; Rom. 1:16; Matt. 5:17, 18; Jude 3; Eph. 1:17, 18; 3:10, 18)[9]

This article restates the position of the shorter IVCF statement but goes further: "The message of the Bible is addressed to all mankind." It is universal. No tribe or nation, no group of people is excluded. And no time is too modern to be under its authority, for God's revelation is "unchangeable" and through it "the Holy Spirit still speaks today." There is no escaping its authority over us.

But for our purposes perhaps the most important part of Article 2 is the affirmation that Scripture can be understood by ordinary people with ordinary intelligence when God illuminates their minds. This illumination is not to be thought of as a great mystical experience that allows us to see the "spiritual" meaning of a text which has a plain reference to ordinary matters, a view I will address specifically in chapter eight. Rather, the Holy Spirit "illumines the minds of God's people in every culture to perceive its truth freshly through their own eyes and thus discloses to the whole church ever more of the many-colored wisdom of God."

Notice: the illumination comes to the minds of "God's people"—not just to the spiritual elite. There is no guru class in biblical Christianity, no illuminati, no people through whom all proper interpretation must come. And so, while the Holy Spirit gives special gifts of wisdom, knowledge and spiritual discernment, he does not assign these gifted Christians to be the only authoritative interpreters of his Word (1 Cor. 12:8-10). It is up to each of his people to learn, to judge and to discern by reference to the Bible which stands as the authority over even those to whom God has given special abilities.

And notice also that the illumination comes to the "minds" of God's people—not to some nonrational faculty like our "emotions" or our "feelings." To know God's revelation means to use our mind. This makes knowledge something we can share with others, something we can talk about. God's Word is in words with ordinary rational content. This point is important, as we shall see in chapter six.

To summarize, the assumption I am making throughout

the entire book is that the Bible is God's true revelation to all humanity, that it is our ultimate authority on all matters about which it speaks, that it is not a total mystery but can be adequately understood by ordinary people in every culture. If the Bible is allowed to speak for itself and not forced into the mold of some foreign preconception, it does not speak ambiguously but clearly on the central matters of human life: Who is God? Who is mankind? Who am I? What is the purpose of life? What is the good life? How should we then live?

A Question of Tone
Before delving into the details of analysis, I would like to address one more general theme—the question of tone. How should we address ourselves to issues which are sometimes emotionally very upsetting?

When we see people misuse the Bible, it hurts us. I think it should hurt us. God's Word is holy, his truth inviolate. We have staked our lives on it. So when it is attacked or co-opted in behalf of error, we suffer.

I think that is why so many Christian books on alternative religions are often so bitter, even nasty, in tone. Cult leaders and followers alike are held up to ridicule as stupid, perverted, demonic, satanic, beneath contempt. Some Christian writers seem to be at fever pitch when they draft their books, articles and tracts.

A seige mentality is at work. Those who hold cultic ideas are seen as the enemy, the great threat to humanity, to Christians, even, some seem to suggest, to God himself. Like Satan they are "like a roaring lion, seeking some one to devour" (1 Pet. 5:8). So in response anything goes: innuendo, name-calling, backhanded remarks, assumption of the worst motives on the part of the cult believers. And thus the Christian dehumanizes the enemy and shoots him like a dog.

But the Christian in this process is himself dehumanized. By treating those whose views are different as no longer made in the image of God, Christians come close to denying in practice their own godlikeness. And as far as effective Christian evangelism is concerned, God's grace alone must account for any conversions from cult to Christianity that ever occur as a result.

Concerning a woman who founded one religious movement, one well-known authority on the cults writes, "George was the only child she ever had. She hardly had him, for he was sent off to school and farmed out with relatives, so that the saying was that Mary did not care for her lamb."[10] Note the loaded language ("the only child she ever *had*. She hardly *had* him") which depersonalizes the mother. She is said to have *farmed* out her child, something you do with livestock. And then comes the cute quip. The author has been clever, but hardly fair.

As readers, especially ones who are not members of the religious movement she founded, we smile. We are pleased that this cult has such a poor specimen of the human race as its founder. But we ought to remember that it is not those outside the influence of the cults that we wish to amuse but those inside we wish to attract and convince.

It is true, of course, that those who are misled by error and who propagate error are not to be followed and should, in fact, be made aware of their position before God. But cult believers and evangelists are still human. And all human beings must be treated with respect. Perhaps we should remember Shylock's retort in *The Merchant of Venice* when he felt maligned by Christians: "If you prick us, do we not bleed? . . . if you poison us, do we not die? and if you wrong us, shall we not revenge?" (III, i, 68-70).

It is important to hold to the truth of the Christian faith in the face of cultic error, but it is equally important to honor the personhood of the cult believer. It will only be by respecting him or her as a person that we will even be able to cast the shadow of doubt over the cult believer's faith. It is not revenge for mistreatment we wish to spark, but doubt in the mind of those in error—doubt that paves the way for truth.

Cult: A Loaded Term

Unfortunately, there is one loaded word that I cannot conveniently avoid. The word *cult* itself is heavy with negative connotations. Imagine a friend you haven't seen for a while greeting you and saying, "Oh, by the way. Last week I joined a cult. Would you like to hear about it?"

In the aftermath of publicity about Jim Jones and the murders and mass suicides in Jonestown, other nontraditional religious movements became nervous. The Unification Church of Sun Myung Moon, for example, often called a *cult* by the media, quickly denounced Jones and tried to disassociate itself from the whole *cult* concept. No one confesses to being a member of a cult. They are followers of a Master, devotees of Krishna, pilgrims on the way—but not cult members.

Should we not honor this feeling and refrain from using a word with such a stigma attached to it? We should, if we could, but we can't. Other terms such as *religion, religious movement, alternative religion* are too general and do not give the sense of exclusivity associated with groups commonly termed cults. A term like *spiritual counterfeit* is even more loaded than *cult*. So I think we are stuck with it.

Still, I want to be clear about the sense in which I will be using the term. For the purposes of this book a *cult* is simply *any religious movement that is organizationally distinct and has doctrines and/or practices that contradict those of the Scriptures as interpreted by traditional Christianity as represented by the major Catholic and Protestant denominations, and as expressed in such statements as the Apostles' Creed.*

In this sense, the Church of Christ, Scientist (Christian Science) is a cult, as is The Unification Church (headed by Sun Myung Moon), the Jehovah's Witnesses, the Latter-day Saints (Mormons) and so forth. Totally non-Christian movements like the International Society for Krishna Consciousness (Hare Krishnas) and Transcendental Meditation (TM) are often not thought of as cults because they originate in another religious tradition. Still, their leaders often quote the Christian Scriptures as if they supported their own doctrine. So for this reason, I will not emphasize their distinction from the Christian-oriented cults. We are interested in how the Scripture is twisted out of shape by anyone, how it is co-opted into the service of essentially non-Christian thought.

The term *cultic* will likewise be used in a general sense to refer to *any idea or practice consistent with any cult's doctrine or lifestyle but not consistent with the Bible's teaching as classically understood by Christians of varied cultures throughout the centuries.*

What the Doctor Ordered
This book began with an odd sensation. But researching and writing it has helped to calm my stomach. It was, you might say, just what the doctor ordered. It is my hope for readers as well that what follows will be effective medicine—if not for calming your stomach, perhaps for curing some of the diseases of misreading that plague us all.

Chapter 2
World-View Confusion: A Preliminary View

In much of the world, especially the Western world, the Bible has been a major source of religious authority. Until a few decades ago if someone wanted to convince you that his particular doctrine was correct, he would try to show you how it was supported by the Scriptures.

Of course, in recent decades that attitude has waned until the Bible itself seems to be in need of defense. Its authority is impugned by secularists and non-Christian religious movements alike. Impugned but by no means destroyed. "The Bible says" was and still is for many people the final authority.[1] And even for many others who make no pretense of being especially religious or devout, reference to the Bible sparks a sacred awe. Much better that a religious idea be found in the Bible than that it be merely the view of some contemporary philosopher, theologian or guru. The Bible is at least the repository of the best insights of our Western ethical and religious heritage. Its comments, while not necessarily absolute truth, are worth more than most other words of wisdom.

A Jesus for Everyone

Even more authoritative, of course, are special parts of the Bible, particularly the words of its key figure. Jesus—that towering and tremendously attractive figure out of our religious past—is still thought of as the ideal man. No, many modern people would say, he was not God, but he was "divine" in some lesser sense; for example, he realized his humanity to the fullest extent. He was what all of us long to be—the perfect, or almost perfect, human being.

Jesus, in fact, is co-opted by almost everyone who wants someone from the past to confirm their own vision of the ideal future. To Eastern-oriented religious groups, Jesus is an avatar—one of the many incarnations of God; to Christian Scientists, he is the Great Healer; to political revolutionaries, he is the Great Liberator; to Spiritualists, he is a first-rate medium; to one new consciousness philosopher, he is the prototype of Carlos Castenada's don Juan, a sorcerer who can restructure events in the world by mental exercise. Everyone, it seems, wants Jesus for themselves.

But—and this is the important point—unless one has a special, unique, new revelation, the only Jesus we can have is the Jesus of the Bible. The Bible is the only source of any extensive knowledge about him. References in other sources are too scanty to be useful to one who wants to make Jesus an advocate of his or her philosophy.

The question is, then, How is the Bible used to support the varying claims of those who want for rhetorical purposes to stand on its authority? This question has many answers. In fact, by my count, it has at least twenty answers. In the following chapters I will examine each one in turn.

The most significant and pervasive explanation of how the Bible is used to support essentially nonbiblical ideas involves *world-view confusion*. Because it is so fundamental to our understanding of the misuse of Scripture, we will examine it twice—first in this chapter and again as Misreading No. 20 in chapter nine.

World-View Confusion: Defined

Let me begin by defining two terms: first, *world view*, and then *world-view confusion*. *A world view is a set of presuppositions (or assumptions) which we hold (consciously or unconsciously) about the basic make-up of our world.*[2] As Alvin Toffler says, "Every person carries in his head a mental model of the world—a subjective representation of external reality."[3] This mental model acts as a giant filing cabinet; it contains a slot for every item of information coming to us.

If, for example, we see a beast approaching us as we are walking down the sidewalk, it is important that we have the mental filing slots for the data that will help us decide whether the beast is a dog or a lion; and if a dog, a friendly or an unfriendly one. Our physical well-being depends on an adequate understanding of the possibilities.

The world flings itself at us in a constant barrage of data—the data of our five senses, the messages of ordinary conversation, of traffic signals, of billboards and books, of radio and television. Our mental and spiritual health depends on having a frame of reference that can sort out the useful from the useless, the meaningful from the meaningless, the trivial from the profound.

The problem is this: when a new idea comes our way, what are we going to do with it? How will we identify and label it so that we can make it a congenial part of our mental furniture? This is an ongoing problem in everyone's life. But it is especially important when dealing with the Bible.

We need to be sure we are correctly understanding its message, for it is God himself who speaks to us through it. In short, we need to avoid *world-view confusion*. And that brings us to the second key term.

World-view confusion occurs whenever a reader of Scripture fails to interpret the Bible within the intellectual and broadly cultural framework of the Bible itself and uses instead a foreign frame of reference. In other words, rather than seeing a statement of Scripture as a part of the whole biblical scheme of things, the reader or interpreter views it from a different standpoint and thus distorts the Bible, perhaps seriously, sometimes even reversing the meaning.

All this discussion has been very abstract. We need a few clear examples.

Paul and Barnabas: Hermes and Zeus

Nowhere is the failure to understand God's message of salvation more clearly illustrated than by an event recorded in the Bible itself. World-view confusion was precisely the problem that arose in Lystra when Paul and Barnabas preached the gospel in that city (Acts 14:8-18).[4] As these two evangelists were speaking, a crippled man, who had never walked, was among the attentive listeners. Paul saw that this man had faith, and so he called to him: "Stand upright on your feet."

When the man jumped up and walked around, the people exclaimed, "The gods have come down to us in the likeness of men!" They mistook Barnabas for Zeus, and Paul they called Hermes "because he was the chief speaker."

The people had made a simple but crucial error. They had interpreted Paul's message and his healing in the framework of their own Greek religion. The priest of Zeus himself encouraged this by bringing flowers and preparing a sacrifice of oxen at the city's temple of Zeus.

Paul and Barnabas were so staggered by this confusion that they took dramatic action to remedy the misconception. They tore their garments to show they were just plain ordinary flesh and blood, and they explained again what they were trying to say earlier: "We also are men, of like nature with you, and bring you good news, that you should turn from these vain things to a living God who made the heaven and the earth and the sea and all that is in them." In other words, they explicitly challenged the world view, the frame of reference, of the Greek people. God is not who they had taken him to be—a pantheon of gods—but the One Living Creator and Lord of the Universe.

The people of Lystra are not alone in their tendency to see God's revelation in terms of their own inadequate understanding. World-view confusion is a serious problem for all of us in reading the Scriptures of the Old and New Testaments. They were written a long time ago by ancient Hebrews. The culture they assume is different from ours. So we must come to the Bible carefully—listening to it, hearing it, opening our minds to its own frame of reference.

Throughout the ensuing chapters we should keep in mind that world-view confusion in some way probably lies behind most other types of misreading. After we have looked at these other more specific types, we will return to world-view confusion, devoting an entire chapter to it.

But before we turn to the finer points of misreading, let me try to set the definition of world-view confusion more firmly by looking at several specific instances. Because the most obvious examples are found where world views are quite different, we will look at three cases in which the Bible is understood in the framework of Eastern spirituality, Eastern pantheistic monism. What I mean by these terms will become clear as we proceed.

Zen and the Art of Biblical Interpretation

Swami Satchitananda, whom I quoted in the preface, interprets Jesus' beatitude, "Blessed are the pure in heart, for they shall see God" (Mt. 5:8) as follows: "Blessed are those who purify their consciousness, for they shall see themselves as God."

Jesus in the context of his own teaching implies a clear distinction between God and any person, even the "pure in heart." The pure in heart, though finite, are blessed by seeing the pure and righteous, infinite God. They are blessed by coming into a personal relationship with him.

Swami Satchitananda, on the other hand, assumes a world view in which there is ultimately no distinction between God and people. Each person is essentially "divine." His point, therefore, is that if we "purify" our consciousness, if we come to experientially realize who we are, we will grasp the fact that our soul is really the soul of the universe; that is, that each of us is God.

We must be aware, however, that now the very definition of the word *God* has changed. Swami Satchitananda's God is not the God of Abraham, Isaac and Jacob and the Father of our Lord Jesus Christ, but rather the impersonal essence of the universe itself. In world-view terms, Satchitananda is a pantheist. Jesus is a theist.

Let us take a second illustration of world-view confusion, this time from a book on Zen. Robert Linssen writes, "Ch'an and Zen require us, as do certain Christian scriptures, to 'die to ourselves.' This is not a physical death but a foregoing of our attachments and our habits. . . . As Chuang Tzu puts it: 'The great man has no longer any self, for he has bound all the parts of his being into one ecstatic contemplation of universal unity.' "[5] Here the Christian notion of putting aside attachments to selfish desire and becoming obedient to Christ is confused with the Zen Buddhist notion of mystical union with ultimate but impersonal reality.[6] To die to self in Christian terms is to die to our sinful selves and be transformed by the Holy Spirit, recreated and restored in God's image (Col. 3:9-10). It is not to be in ecstacy as one contemplates universal unity. The systems have been confused.

A third illustration, this time from a Hindu orientation, will be our last until we take up the topic in detail. In his introduction to the Upanishads, Juan Mascaro writes, "The doctrine of the *Upanishads* explains and complements the doctrine of the Gospels, 'Thou shalt love thy neighbor as thyself' [Mt. 22:39]. Why? Because our Atman, our higher Self, dwells in us and dwells in our neighbor: if we love our neighbor, we love the God who is in us all and in whom we all are; and if we hurt our neighbor, in thought or in words or in deeds, we hurt ourselves, we hurt our soul: this is the law of spiritual gravitation."[7] But the Upanishads do not complement the doctrine of the Gospels; they contradict that doctrine. The reason we are to love our neighbor—apart from the fact that God has commanded us to do so—is that our neighbor, like us, is created in God's image. He and we are *like* God; and, like God, we love others. In the Upanishads, on the contrary, he and we *are* God; and, being god, we simply love ourselves. In the Upanishads the ethics of love is essentially egocentric; in Christianity the ethics of love is exocentric. It is others whom we love, not for our sake but for theirs.

In all of the above illustrations of world-view confusion the major distinction between the two world views is the notion of what constitutes ultimate or prime reality. The Buddhists and Hindus quoted above both say prime reality is impersonal and essentially a unity, One. All of whatever is real is a part of that unity—a piece of the cosmic action, so to speak. The Christian and Hebrew Scriptures, however, see God as transcendent, the Creator of the cosmos, but separate from it. God spoke the world into being, not making it out of himself by extending his essence, but bringing it into existence *ex nihilo*—out of nothing.

These two basic notions so permeate the two systems in question—Eastern pantheistic monism and Christian theism—that texts drawn from one tradition can frequently not be removed from that tradition and placed in the other without severe distortion. As readers and interpreters of religious texts, therefore, it is incumbent upon us to recognize the difference between the various systems, the various world views, and to interpret these texts first with reference to the system they imply. Failure to do this constitutes world-view confusion.[8]

Multiple Misreading

As we examine each of the various methodological mistakes which follow we will see numerous examples of world-view confusion; the other errors are often merely subspecies of this one large category.

Why, for example, does Linssen not give the biblical texts for "die to ourselves"? Is it to keep us from examining the biblical context in which the phrase appears? This would involve Linssen in *ignoring the immediate context* (Misreading No. 4). Why in so many religious texts and discussions do we find the Bible mined for a phrase here, a sentence there, a verse from Proverbs, a single saying of Jesus? Primarily, I think, because the writer or speaker is working from a nonbiblical frame of reference and is *selectively citing* (Misreading No. 11) to give credibility to his own argument, his own world view.

World-view confusion likewise accounts for *twisted translation* (Misreading No. 2), *inaccurate quotation* (Misreading No. 1), *collapsing contexts* (Misreading No. 5) and so forth.

But this is to jump ahead. We are now ready to take up each type of misreading in detail.

Chapter 3
The Text of Scripture

If we are to understand the Bible—or any work of literature—we must have an accurate text. When the literature is in our own language, the text we read should be the authoritative one—the one the author and publisher agreed was, at least for that edition, the best possible. With most contemporary literature, this is no problem.

If the work to be read is not originally in our native language, then we need more help. We should either learn that language or entrust ourselves to the best translations available and, perhaps, secure a few commentaries by scholars who have studied the original and can help us over the difficulties, if any, in the translation.

Without a reliable text or accurate translation, error is bound to arise. In this chapter we will look at two ways the cults misrepresent what the text of Scripture actually is.

Misreading No. 1: Inaccurate Quotation
Sometimes those in the cults simply misquote the Bible. For example, Jess Stearn in a book on Edgar Cayce quotes the following conversation he had with Eula Allen, one of Cayce's followers. The topic was reincarnation and Stearn suddenly thought of a problem:

A thought struck me. "Why, if people have lived other lives, don't they remember anything from them?"

"But they do," she said. "It's just sometimes that they don't remember that they are remembering. Jesus said, 'I'll bring all things to thine remembrance,' but he didn't say how."[1]

A number of errors are made here. First, this is not what Jesus said. Let us put the clause quoted into its immediate context. Jesus has been talking intimately to his closest followers in the Upper Room, just prior to his crucifixion. His remarks in this setting are profound and moving. Then he says, "These things have I spoken unto you, being yet present with you. But the Comforter, which is the Holy Ghost, whom the Father will send in my name, he shall teach you all things, and bring all things to your remembrance, whatsoever I have said unto you" (Jn. 14:25-26 KJV). As we can see, Jesus did not say *he* would "bring all things to thine remembrance." He said that the *Holy Spirit* would do that. So the quotation is itself inaccurate.

Worse, the phrase following the quoted clause, clearly explains just what would be remembered—"whatsoever I [Jesus] have said unto you [the disciples]." There is not only no *hint* of information about the disciples' past lives, there is an explicit identification of what they would recall— Jesus' teaching. Moreover, the words were not addressed to a general audience of men and women but to his closest friends. These words were not meant for us but for those in the Upper Room.

The point of this illustration is that the Bible is not always quoted accurately. So, if you are confronted by someone who quotes the Bible, check to see if that basic claim is true. Does the Bible say what the person says it does?

The following example is slightly more subtle. In a talk Edgar Cayce once gave, he said, "Jesus said that the whole gospel is 'Thou shalt love the Lord thy God with all thy heart, thy soul, and thy body, and thy neighbor as thyself.' Then all the rest of the Bible is nothing but an explanation of that one sentence."[2] The quotation is a rough but fair rendering of the biblical text (Mk. 12:30-31; Mt. 22:37-39),[3] but the nature of the topic under discussion is misidentified. Jesus was not summarizing the gospel (the good news). Far from it. He was giving the essence of the law. Here is the full passage as it appears in the Gospel according to Matthew:

> Then one of them, which was a lawyer, asked him a question, tempting him, and saying, Master, which is the great commandment in the law? Jesus said unto him, Thou shalt love the Lord thy God with all thy heart, and with all thy soul, and with all thy mind. This is the first and great commandment. And the second is like unto it, Thou shalt love thy neighbour as thyself. On these two commandments hang all the law and the prophets. (Mt. 22:35-40 KJV)

These two commands, however, are not the good news because no one can keep them. People are fallen and simply incapable of loving either God or others with all their heart, soul and body. In a real sense, these commands are the bad news: that is, God demands of us more than we can give.

The gospel, on the other hand, is the good news that Jesus died for our sins. God in Jesus provided for the fact that we cannot keep this law. Contrary to Cayce, therefore, the "rest of the Bible" is a great deal more than an explanation of "that one sentence."

Again, we note that this cultic use of Scripture begins with an inaccurate text. And again, more of the context of the original would have prevented Cayce's easy molding of the passage to fit his preconceived system.

As a third illustration of misquoting, can you see what is wrong with the following comment from the Maharishi Mahesh Yogi, founder of Transcendental Meditation? "Christ said, 'Be still and know that I am God.' Be still and know that you are God and when you know that you are God you will begin to live Godhood, and living Godhood there is no reason to suffer."[4] Of course, more than misquoting is involved. We will be discussing other problems in this passage later (pp. 42 and 52-54). In any case, the original meaning of the clause itself is completely lost.

Misreading No. 2: Twisted Translation
To get at the meaning of the Bible, we need to have an accurate text. If there are errors in the text before us, we are bound to be misled. Some religious movements have addressed this problem by providing their own translations. Current translations, they hold, are inaccurate in some crucial aspects. The fact is, of course, that no single translation or group of translations are beyond improvement. That is why scholars in every generation, especially since the Reformation, have worked to provide an ever more reliable Greek and Hebrew text, and why translators have been at work as well to turn this text into more and more accurate vernacular translations. Cult translations, however, often seem made more to provide a biblical basis for cultic doctrine than to render the best texts accurately.

Case 1. The Jehovah's Witnesses, for example, in 1961 completed their translation of the entire Bible—the New World Translation of the Holy Scriptures (NWT). Consider its rendering of Colossians 1:15-17, where the opening pronoun refers to Christ.

He is the image of the invisible God, the first-born of all creation; because by means of him all [other] things were created in the heavens and upon the earth, the things visible and the things invisible, no matter whether they are thrones or lordships or governments or authorities. All [other] things have been created through him and for him. Also, he is before all [other] things and by means of him all [other] things were made to exist.

This translation compares closely with other, more widely recognized translations, except for the four occurrences of the word *other* in brackets. "Brackets," we are told in the Foreword to the translation, "enclose words inserted to complete or clarify the sense in the English text."[5] By inserting the word *other*, however, the translators have not merely "completed" or "clarified" the English translation, they have altered the meaning of the original. Why? A look at the Jehovah's Witnesses doctrines of the Bible and of God and Jesus soon reveals the answer.

"The Holy Scriptures of the Bible are the standard by which to judge all religions," says one Witness publication.[6] And in *"Let God Be True,"* a popular book teaching Jehovah's Witnesses doctrine, we find this: "To let God be true . . . means to accept his Word, the Bible, as the truth."[7] In this the Jehovah's Witnesses parallel the view of traditional Christianity. So, like traditional Christians, Witnesses wish to submit themselves to the teachings of Scripture.

But—and here is the problem—Jehovah's Witnesses deny the doctrine of the Trinity and the coequality of God the Father, God the Son and God the Holy Spirit, holding instead a "modern form of the ancient heresy of Arianism."[8] Christ, they believe, was created by God as a spirit-creature named Michael. Then through Christ God made all other created things. Therefore, if Scripture is to fit preconceived doctrine, Colossians 1:15-17 needs

"clarification," to wit, "amending." Otherwise the Bible is
here declaring that Christ is *before all things* and in fact was
involved in the creation of all things. It would, in short,
make him coeternal with God.

But—it is fair to ask—is there any warrant in the Greek
text for insertion of the word *other?* If there is, we should
clearly include it. Metzger responds, "It is not present in
the original Greek and was obviously inserted to make the
passage refer to Jesus as being on a par with other created
things." Metzger goes on to point out that Paul originally
wrote Colossians in part to combat a notion of Christ similar to that held by the Jehovah's Witnesses: "Some of the
Colossians advocated the Gnostic notion that Jesus was the
first of many other created intermediaries between God
and men."[9] We can conclude, therefore, that the Jehovah's
Witnesses have deliberately altered a key biblical text that
would—on the basis of their own view of the authority of
the Bible—serve to contradict one of their distinctive doctrines. Metzger notes six other passages which the NWT
also twists to a form more congenial to Witness doctrine:
John 1:1, Philippians 2:6, Titus 2:13, 2 Peter 1:1, Revelation 3:14 and Proverbs 8:22. We will examine their translation of John 1:1 later (pp. 139-40 and 161-64).[10]

Case 2. The Mormons have also altered the text of Scripture by what they call translation, for they, like the Jehovah's Witnesses, claim to base their doctrines on the
Bible. Unlike the Witnesses, however, they add three other
works to their canon of Scripture: "We believe the Bible
to be the word of God as far as it is translated correctly;
we also believe the Book of Mormon to be the word of
God" (Article 8 of the Mormon Articles of Faith). To
these they also append the *Doctrine and Covenants* and the
Pearl of Great Price.[11]

One phrase is of special interest to us now: "We believe
the Bible to be the word of God *as far as it is translated cor-*

rectly." When traditional Christians point out the inconsistency between Mormon doctrine and the Bible, the typical Mormon response is, "But there are many errors in the Bible because it has been corrupted in transmission and in translation." Central to Mormon teaching is the idea that soon after Jesus died his true followers were unable to maintain the purity of Jesus' teaching. The Bible we have was so affected by the apostasy of the church that it is no longer reliable.[12] Thus there was need for a new revelation which would clarify and purify the teaching of the church. This revelation came to Joseph Smith via angelic visitations and a set of golden plates which God helped Smith translate into the Book of Mormon. Other revelations such as those in the *Doctrine and Covenants* 93 (which claims to be "a revelation given through Joseph Smith the prophet, at Kirtland, Ohio, May 6, 1833") quote, comment on and radically change phrases out of John's Gospel, especially the first chapter. This we shall examine in more detail later (see pp. 102-03 and 141-43).

The Bible itself, however, still remains as the first authority in the list of four. And Joseph Smith himself undertook to translate it correctly.[13] The result has been published by the Reorganized Church of Jesus Christ of Latter-day Saints (headquartered in Independence, Missouri), a group which broke from the main body in 1844. A part of this translation also appears in the Book of Moses section of the *Pearl of Great Price.* Smith's version, however, is far from a translation.

The opening chapter of Genesis, for example, is recast as a direct revelation to Moses: "The words of God, which he spake unto Moses at a time when Moses was caught up into an exceedingly high mountain.... And God spake unto Moses, saying: Behold, I am the Lord God Almighty, and Endless is my name ... " (Moses 1:1, 3). The creation is not taken up until Moses 2. Here God continues to speak in the first person: "Behold, I reveal unto you concerning this heaven, and this earth; write the words which I speak. I am the Beginning and the End, the Almighty God; by mine Only Begotten I created these things; yea, in the beginning I created the heaven, and the earth upon which thou standest" (Moses 2:1). There is no question of this being a translation in any ordinary sense of the term. This is rather new revelation altering old revelation supposedly because the only original-language texts we have have been too corrupted to be reliable.

The result is that Mormons are asked to believe Joseph Smith's revealed "translation" which cannot be checked against any manuscripts at all. Readers who are curious about the reliability of the New and Old Testament manuscripts on which contemporary translations such as the Revised Standard Version (RSV) and New International Version (NIV) are based may wish to consult F. F. Bruce, *The New Testament Documents: Are They Reliable?* and K. A. Kitchen, *Ancient Orient and Old Testament.*[14]

I conclude this section by simply repeating my major points. To interpret the Bible accurately we need to have an accurate translation before us. When a cult believer calls into question the standard versions available today, we need to look twice to see what is being claimed. Not all new translations are misleading; and even the NWT can be used effectively to present the gospel to Jehovah's Witnesses because much of it is sufficiently accurate to be, if not a testimony against their doctrine, at least a conveyor of the basic gospel message. John 3:16, for example, is still intact.

Our responsibility as Christians is to test cultic translations to see if they are reasonably accurate. We may need help on this matter if we are not experts in Greek and Hebrew. But such help is usually not far away. Our local church pastor can often put us on the right track. Then, too, the translation used may be adequate but misquoted.

Does the Bible really say that? This should be our first question in responding to teaching allegedly based on Scripture.

Chapter 4
Scripture as Rhetoric

T he Bible has long been a book that commands attention. If you can employ it in the service of your own cause,
you can gain for your cause a certain credibility—even
where the Bible is not accepted as the sole authority on
matters of faith and life. It is this situation that explains
the misuse of Scripture discussed in this chapter: Scripture
employed primarily for rhetorical purposes.

Misreading No. 3: The Biblical Hook
When Scripture is quoted, especially at the beginning of an
argument which turns out to promote a cult doctrine or
point of view, it may be that it is being used primarily as a
hook to grasp the attention of readers or listeners. "The
Bible says" gets the attention, but what follows the quotation may be far from traditional Christian teaching and far

from the intention of the Bible itself.

One of the major rhetorical uses of the Bible or any source of "high quality quotes" such as Shakespeare, Homer or Dante (or even such modern writers as Dostoevsky, C. S. Lewis or Francis Schaeffer!) is as a pretext for one's own ideas. A handy phrase comes to mind and we use it, never looking up its original context or caring one whit about what it originally meant.

Some Christian preachers are well known, unfortunately, for their own similar use of the Bible. The preacher wants to say something to his congregation, so he looks for a verse or two of Scripture on which to hang his preconceived message.

This, I think, partially explains the Maharishi Mahesh Yogi's use of Psalm 46:10 already quoted (see p. 34). When the Maharishi follows "Be still and know that I am God" with "Be still and know that you are God," he is not concerned for the original meaning of the text. These words are a pretext for his own peculiar teaching, in this case a teaching diametrically opposed to the meaning of the original.

The Biblical Hook and Mormon Apologetics
On a much more sophisticated level the Mormons use such an approach in their door-to-door evangelistic work. The Mormon missionary's first goal is to schedule a time to present a several-week series of instruction in Mormon doctrine to an entire family. Once this has been arranged in a pleasant, comfortable way, the missionary's task is to lead the family into the details of the Mormon religion, the ultimate goal being the family's entry into the Church of Jesus Christ of Latter-day Saints by baptism.

The topic of the first session is "The Restoration" in which the main idea is that the traditional churches have distorted true religion and that God has through the

Prophet Joseph Smith and the Book of Mormon "restored" purity to his church. In the words of the missionary manual, "The Lord has shown his love and concern for us in our time by appearing to a prophet, revealing the Book of Mormon, and restoring his Church with his authority and power. One can discover the truth of these things by reading and pondering the Book of Mormon and praying sincerely."[1]

To present this general idea the missionary opens the discussion by reading from Joseph Smith's account of his early disillusionment with traditional Christianity and his steadfast search for the truth. He had tried the various churches in his area, he says, but each one was at odds with the others. "So great were the confusion and strife among the different denominations, that it was impossible for a person young as I was [fifteen years old, he says], and so unacquainted with men and things, to come to any certain conclusion who was right and who was wrong."[2] It was during the frustration of this situation that, Smith says, "I was one day reading the Epistle of James, first chapter and fifth verse, which reads: 'If any of you lack wisdom, let him ask of God, that giveth to all men liberally, and upbraideth not; and it shall be given him.' Never did any passage of Scripture come with more power to the heart of man than this did at this time to mine." Smith says that he mulled over these words in his mind, realizing that "if any person needed wisdom from God, he did ... ; for the teachers of religion of the different sects understood the same passages of Scripture so differently as to destroy all confidence in settling the question by an appeal to the Bible."

So, following the words of James 1:5, Smith went directly to God for the answer. In the spring of 1820 on a "beautiful, clear day," he went into the woods, "kneeled down and began to offer up the desire of my heart to God." As he was praying, Smith says, "I saw a pillar of light exactly over my head, above the brightness of the sun which descended gradually until it fell upon me. . . . When the light rested upon me I saw two personages, whose brightness and glory defy all description, standing above me in the air. One of them spake unto me, calling me by name and said, pointing to the other—*'This is my Beloved Son. Hear Him!'*"

After sharing this portion of Smith's story with the family, the missionary asks the father of the family (he is called Mr. Brown in the missionary's manual) to imagine himself in Smith's position. Would not he, too, be over-whelmed? Then the missionary suggests that Mr. Brown can have the same assurance about the truth of God as Joseph Smith. This thought is not, however, developed until near the end of the session. Instead, the missionary emphasizes that Smith was told to join none of the churches because they were apostate. Then the missionary tells the family the story of the origin of the Book of Mormon and testifies that this new revelation is the word of God. Smith himself, they learn, was appointed as a priest and prophet in God's new restored church, a church which today still has a living prophet at its head. By association with this restored church Mr. Brown and his family can receive "the full blessings of the kingdom of God."[3]

The family is then asked to read a pamphlet containing Joseph Smith's testimony and some specific passages of the Book of Mormon. It is at this point that the implication of James 1:5 as understood by Smith is driven home. The missionary is to say, "The Lord wants us to understand that the way to know the truth of anything is to ask God, just as Joseph Smith did," and to read the following passage from the Book of Mormon:

Behold, I would exhort you that when ye shall read these things, if it be wisdom in God that ye should read them, that ye would remember how merciful the Lord hath been unto the children of men, from the creation of Adam even down unto the time that ye shall receive these things and ponder it in your hearts.

And when ye shall receive these things, I would exhort you that ye would ask God, the Eternal Father, in the name of Christ, if these things be true; and if ye shall ask with a sincere heart, with real intent, having faith in Christ, he will manifest the truth of it to you, by the power of the Holy Ghost.

And by the power of the Holy Ghost ye may know the truth of all things. (Moroni 10:3-5)

These verses are the key text for Mormon apologetics. Ask most Mormons why they believe the Book of Mormon, or any Mormon teaching, and the response is most likely to be, "I sincerely prayed and asked God to tell me if the Book of Mormon is true. He has confirmed this in my heart." As the missionary is to say to Mr. Brown, "I know you will feel the truth of our message if you will make the effort to ponder these things and will seek the Lord in prayer."[4]

This is, of course, a totally subjective apologetic. The only evidence is that given in one's own mind or heart and in the minds and hearts of other Mormons. And, while Mormon scholar James E. Talmage gives several more objective "proofs" for the Book of Mormon, even he concludes, "There is promised a surer and more effectual means of ascertaining the truth or falsity of this volume. Like other scriptures, the Book of Mormon is to be comprehended through the spirit of scripture, and this is obtainable only as a gift from God. But this gift is promised to all who seek it." Then he quotes Moroni 10:4-5, the passage quoted above.[5]

God the Father: A New Revelation

By now Christian readers may wish to pause for analysis

and reflection. But I would like to add one factor before we stand back to ponder the Mormon argument. Immediately following the challenge to Mr. Brown to sincerely pray for God's wisdom in discerning the truth of Mormon scripture, the missionary closes session one by presenting an important distinctive feature of Mormon doctrine: "God and Jesus Christ are separate and distinct persons, each with a glorified and perfected body of flesh and bones."[6]

When as traditional Christians we hear this doctrine for the first time, we may suddenly be shocked or at least confused. "God the Father has a body? How did Joseph Smith ever get that idea?" How did he get from the perfectly orthodox James 1:5 to the grossly heretical notion that God the Father has a body of flesh and bones? Doesn't John 4:24 clearly say, 'God is spirit'?"[7]

Such shocked Christian skepticism is well founded. Joseph Smith's vision does not square with the picture of God the Father given in the Bible. Neither Jewish nor Christian scholars, nor for that matter secular scholars of the Bible, read the Bible like the Mormons must do to bring it into line with Smith's conclusion. (We will look later at some of the ways Mormons employ Scripture to substantiate their theology: see pp. 59-61, 68-74, 101-04, 140-43.)

What concerns us now, however, is the *biblical hook*. The Mormon missionary uses Smith's supposed recognition of the Bible's authority to authenticate a vision and a doctrine that are clearly nonbiblical. The story as Smith tells it puts Smith in a very favorable light. He proclaims himself to be an honest seeker after ultimate truth. He searches for this truth in the standard places—the Christian churches. These churches confuse him and cause him to conclude that the Bible cannot be understood well enough on its own. Then his eyes light on James 1:5, and Smith (this time able somehow to understand the Bible for himself) follows its promise: "If any of you lack wisdom, let him ask of God, that giveth to all men liberally.... " When he receives the vision of God the Father and God the Son, he receives God's promised gift of wisdom. What could be wrong with this sequence of events, this "argument" whose conclusion must be that God has a body?

As traditional Christians, the first thing we notice is that what Smith "learned" is contradictory to the Bible. Because we accept the Bible as our authority, we can be confident that Smith, even if the story he tells of his vision is true to his experience, has drawn the wrong conclusions from it. We can be confident that Smith is in error here because we are reminded of two verses which Smith does not refer to: "But though we, or *an angel from heaven,* preach any other gospel unto you than that which we have preached unto you, let him be accursed. As we said before, so say I now again, If any *man* preach any other gospel unto you than that ye have received, let him be accursed" (Gal. 1:8-9 KJV).[8] The apostle Paul is here declaring that the gospel cannot be changed; what once was true is still true. The witness of the Bible is against the notion that God the Father has a body. If it was not true in New Testament times, it is not true now.[9]

In both the Old and New Testaments we are asked over and over to discern false teaching from true, and we are asked to do so on the basis of earlier revelation. Does what is taught fit with what God has said previously? See in the Old Testament, for example, the trial of Jeremiah for false prophecy (Jer. 26). He was acquitted, for even though he spoke hard words against Jerusalem, they were consistent with those of the earlier prophet Micah. The point here is that the Mormons use James 1:5 as a platform on which to erect two false ideas: (1) that God has a body and (2) that people today can know that Mormon teaching is true by simply praying and waiting for a sense of confirmation in their heart or mind. Or to return to the image used earlier, the Mormons use James 1:5 to hook the reader, and, once hooked, drag him into nonbiblical teaching.

True Wisdom: James 1:5 Revisited
In all of this we have yet to do what every serious student of the Bible must do: look at the text in context. First, what does *wisdom* in James 1:5 mean in relation to its immediate context in the letter of James? Second, what does *wisdom* mean in the larger context of both the New and the Old Testaments?

Within the framework of James the passage sets the tone and subject of the entire letter. James is a book of wisdom —that is, a book of advice and admonishment. The remainder of the letter is, in one sense, a long answer to the question of what is meant by *wisdom* in 1:5. One thing is clearly not in evidence in James—any notion that one receives wisdom by visions or any other solely subjective experience like a warm feeling in the heart.

In the larger context of the Bible, especially the Old Testament, *wisdom* is seen as "intensely practical, not theoretical. Basically wisdom is the art of being successful, of forming the correct plan to gain the desired results."[10] In the New Testament also wisdom has an "intensely practical nature." Furthermore, "If divorced from God's revelation [the Old and New Testaments] it is impoverished and unproductive at best... and foolish or even devilish at worst."[11] In short the concept of wisdom does not so much emphasize the notion of knowledge as of ability to use knowledge in a practical way to best advantage.

It is clear that Smith interprets the wisdom of James 1:5 in a rather different fashion. It means for him the ability to know God truly apart from biblical revelation (which is too uncertain and open to too many interpretations to be trustworthy). In other words the *wisdom* of James and the rest of the Bible is not the *wisdom* of Joseph Smith. The unwary reader, however, may not know this, being hooked by the seeming biblical basis for the new revelation of Smith.

A Second Hook

James 1:5 is not the only *biblical hook* used in the argument. The very words of one of the personages in the vision is a direct parallel to the words which came "out of the cloud" at the Transfiguration. Referring to Jesus, the voice said, "This is my beloved Son: hear him" (Mk. 9:7 KJV). Moreover, Jesus himself was "transfigured before them. And his raiment became shining, exceeding white as snow" (Mk. 9:2-3 KJV). Smith's "two personages, whose brightness and glory defy description" parallel Mark's description of Jesus.

But here the parallel ends, for the "voice out of the cloud" identifies Jesus of Nazareth as his Son, and Jesus of Nazareth, that is the Jesus of the Bible, reveals doctrine different from that deriving from Smith's vision. For Jesus of Nazareth said, "God is spirit" (Jn. 4:24). So again, the parallels to the Transfiguration are acting as a biblical hook to pull the unwary not toward the Bible but toward cultic ideas and practices.

Avoiding the Hook

As cautious Christians, we may ask, how can we keep ourselves from being hooked by sophisticated but essentially misleading arguments based on Scripture? The answer is not far away. We should model our lives on the pattern of the Jews in Beroea. Paul and Silas had been teaching in Thessalonica but were forced to leave quickly at night because of opposition. When they arrived at Beroea, they went to the synagogue. "Now these Jews were more noble than those in Thessalonica, for they received the word with all eagerness, examining the scriptures daily to see if these things were so. Many of them therefore believed, with not a few Greek women of high standing as well as men" (Acts 17:11-12).

Joseph Smith abandoned too quickly his quest to find truth from the Scripture. We may well sympathize with fifteen-year-olds who find parts of the Bible baffling, but not with Smith's easy capitulation to extrabiblical revelation as a norm. If we find ourselves in the situation he describes before his vision, frustrated because we can't seem to get a handle on God's truth, our response should be to pray for God's wisdom—yes, indeed—but to apply ourselves again to Scripture and to resist either personal visions proclaiming nonbiblical truth or teaching from others based on such visions. The Bible should only hook us to study more intently the Bible itself. To be hooked on Scripture is to be hooked on truth.

Chapter 5
Scripture as Literature

It seems too obvious to mention, but it is very important for a good reader to recognize that the Bible is literature. That is, the writers of Scripture used normal literary forms for recording revelation. Or, to put it in another way, God chose to reveal himself to us by speaking through his prophets in ordinary language. The rules for understanding the Bible are therefore essentially the same as the rules for understanding Homer, Aeschylus, Dante, Milton, Dickens and Conrad. We are to read in the same spirit as the writer who wrote. If the author wrote a letter, we are to read it as a letter; if a poem, as poetry; if a chronicle, as chronicle; if a parable, as parable; if prophecy, as prophecy.

A host of errors can be avoided simply by realizing the kind of literature each portion of the Bible actually is. If we recognize that Jesus' story of the sower and the seed is a parable, we will not spend our time looking for the field in Palestine to which Jesus was referring. On the other hand, if we recognize that John is narrating an actual event in John 4, we may be helped by picturing the scene in our mind's eye and recapturing the drama of an actual event in Jesus' life. We may even be able to find the place where the well was located when Jesus spoke to the Samaritan woman. Certainly we will not first interpret the well in a spiritual fashion. And, since Jesus himself used the water in the well as a figure for spiritual life, we will not interpret this water in any way contradictory to Jesus' own teaching. To do so would be to lift the well and its water out of its literary context and so lose any authority our interpretation might otherwise have.

But this is to talk theoretically about what *might* happen when we ignore the fact that the Bible is literature. What actually has happened when this was done? In this chapter we will look at six reading errors which stem from failure to take the literary character of God's Word into account.

Misreading No. 4: Ignoring the Immediate Context
From the standpoint of the Bible as literature, the simplest error of reading is the failure to consider the immediate context of the verse or passage in question. The literature of the cults is filled with illustrations of this basic mistake.

Case 1. We have already seen how the Maharishi Mahesh Yogi misquoted Scripture when he attributed the words of Psalm 46:10 to Christ (see p. 42). But in his remarks the Maharishi also ignores the immediate context of the words themselves. "Christ said, 'Be still and know that I am God.' Be still and know that you are God and when you know that you are God you will begin to live Godhood, and living Godhood there is no reason to suffer."[1] A reading of Psalm 46 quickly reveals that "Be still, and know that I am God" is spoken by the Lord God of Israel. In fact, even

the most immediate context—the remainder of verse 10
and verse 11—shows this is so.

"Be still, and know that I am God.
  I am exalted among the nations,
  I am exalted in the earth!"
The LORD of hosts is with us;
  the God of Jacob is our refuge.[2]

With the Maharishi's reading the sense of the original is
not only lost but reversed. The Maharishi is, of course,
writing from a pantheistic frame of reference. All of reality
—including every person—is ultimately divine. It is quite
consistent, therefore, for the Maharishi to advise his
readers to be still (meditate) and know that they are God.

To the Hebrew psalmist, however, and indeed to every
Bible writer, every orthodox Jew and every Christian, such
a thought is not only wrong but blasphemous. "Hear, O
Israel: The LORD our God is one LORD; and you shall
love the LORD your God with all your heart, and with all
your soul, and with all your might" (Deut. 6:4). This first
and greatest commandment (Mk. 12:29-30) requires a distinction between God and man, between Creator and created, between the Origin of all reality and any person (man,
woman or child) made in God's image. To set oneself up
as God, to pretend even for a moment it might be so, is to
commit the most basic of all sins: the primal sin, the original
sin committed by Adam and Eve at the beginning of human
history (Gen. 3:5-6).

But we do not need to set the Maharishi's reading of
"Be still and know that I am God" in the larger context
of the Old and New Testaments to avoid the Maharishi's
mistake. Even a casual reading of the immediate context of
Psalm 46 would prevent such an error. To demonstrate
for yourself that this is so, read the entire psalm.

God is our refuge and strength,
  a very present help in trouble.

Therefore we will not fear though the earth
    should change,
   though the mountains shake in the heart of the sea;
though its waters roar and foam,
   though the mountains tremble with its tumult. *Selah*
There is a river whose streams make glad the city of God,
   the holy habitation of the Most High.
God is in the midst of her, she shall not be moved;
   God will help her right early.
The nations rage, the kingdoms totter;
   he utters his voice, the earth melts.
The LORD of hosts is with us;
   the God of Jacob is our refuge. *Selah*
Come, behold the works of the LORD,
   how he has wrought desolations in the earth.
He makes wars cease to the end of the earth;
   he breaks the bow, and shatters the spear,
   he burns the chariots with fire!
"Be still, and know that I am God.
   I am exalted among the nations,
   I am exalted in the earth!"
The LORD of hosts is with us;
   the God of Jacob is our refuge. *Selah*

Now reread the psalm and ask yourself: What evidence is there that the speaker of verse 10 is a human being? What evidence is there that the Lord of hosts is the speaker? What evidence is there that the Lord of hosts is distinct from human beings? What relationships between the Lord of hosts and various groups of human beings are mentioned? In the context, does "Be still" have anything to do with meditation? What kind of stillness is being talked about? How, then, does the immediate context of "Be still, and know that I am God" affect your understanding of these words?

Case 2. In a very different sort of discourse, we find

Edgar Cayce quoting the Scriptures out of context. Cayce, well known as the Sleeping Prophet, gave many "readings," in which he would first fall asleep and then give information about such matters as the spirit world, the history of the universe and the past lives of people. He could also diagnose diseases and prescribe remarkably accurate cures.

In a "reading" in which the topic of reincarnation was addressed—apparently a frequent occurrence, he was asked if he knew when he might again be reincarnated. Jess Stearn comments and quotes Cayce:

As for the time of his return, Cayce was vague. "It may be perhaps a hundred, two hundred, three hundred, a thousand years, as you may count time in the present. For How gave He [Christ]? The day no man knoweth, only the Father in heaven knoweth, and it is provided you so live, as He gave, that 'I may sit upon the right hand and my brother on the left.' "[3]

Two separate texts of Scripture are here quoted. "The day no man knoweth, only the Father in heaven knoweth" is a rough rendering of Jesus' words in Matthew 24:36 (or the parallels in Mk. 13:32 and Acts 1:7). "I may sit upon the right hand and my brother on the left" is a rough transcription of the request of two of Jesus' disciples to share a special place in Jesus' future kingdom (Mk. 10:37 or the parallel in Mt. 20:21), but the personal pronouns have been changed from "we" (Mk. 10:37) and "these my two sons" (Mt. 20:21) to "I ... and my brother." Yet these textual oddities are minor compared to what Cayce seems to be making the texts say.

Neither text could possibly refer to the topic Cayce was addressing—his own future reincarnation. The context shows that the *day* that only the Father knows is the time of Jesus' Second Coming, an event which in no way involves reincarnation, either Jesus' or Cayce's or anyone's. Cayce has simply plucked words from Scripture and filled them

with his own content. Cayce has collapsed the separate
contexts of the two texts (we will discuss this immediately
below under Misreading No. 5) but not provided enough
of a context of his own for much other than confusion to
result.

Case 3. A remarkably extreme case of *ignoring the immediate context* occurs in *Beyond Theology* by Alan Watts.
Throughout this volume Watts attacks traditional Christian
theology and reinterprets biblical texts to suit his own world
view. In one brief section Watts makes some apt comments
about the way many people want to co-opt Jesus for themselves: "For we are spiritually paralyzed by the fetish of
Jesus. Even to atheists he is the supremely good man, the
exemplar and moral authority with whom no one may disagree. Whatever our opinions, we must perforce wangle
the words of Jesus to agree with them."[4] So far Watts is
echoing the thoughts of many who see Jesus twisted so out
of shape as to be almost unrecognizable.

But Watts goes on, "Poor Jesus! If he had known how
great an authority was to be projected upon him, he would
never have said a word. His literary image in the gospels
has, through centuries of homage, become far more of an
idol than anything graven in wood or stone, so that today
the most genuinely reverent act of worship is to destroy
that image."

At this point, we might note, Watts has gone well beyond
what Christians would want to say. The fact is that the
Jesus of the Gospels is a Jesus of tremendous authority.
That authority has not been projected on him by "centuries
of homage" but has been recognized as central to his character by people down through the ages. The only picture
of Jesus we get is the one in the New Testament. That
is, in Watts's terms the only historical image we have of
Jesus is "his literary image in the gospels." Any other Jesus
is pure speculation. And the Jesus of the Gospels is even

more authoritative than any extrabiblical writing could imagine, for in the Gospels Jesus speaks with such authority that no one can begin to hold their own with him, as the many encounters recorded between him and the Pharisees indicate. The one who said, "I do nothing on my own authority but speak thus as the Father taught me. . . . I always do what is pleasing to him" (Jn. 8:28-29) and "I and the Father are one" (Jn. 10:30), was not exactly a retiring wallflower. Unlike the Buddha who put no stock in words, Jesus had "the words of eternal life." And Peter declared, "We have believed, and have come to know, that you are the Holy One of God" (Jn. 6:68-69).

But let us hear out Watts, for Watts himself uses the Gospel of John to substantiate his claim that we should break the image of the authoritative Jesus.

In his [Jesus'] own words, "It is expedient that I go away, for if I go not away, the Paraclete (the Holy Spirit) cannot come unto you." Or as the angel said to the disciples who came looking for the body of Jesus in the tomb, "Why do you seek the living among the dead? He is risen and gone before you. . . . " But Christian piety does not let him go away, and continues to seek the living Christ in the dead letter of the historical record. As he said to the Jews, "You search the Scriptures, for in them you *think* you have eternal life."[5]

The three texts Watts quotes are, as I suspect most readers will have recognized, lifted completely from their original contexts. The first, John 16:7, is a straightforward promise that the Holy Spirit will come to God's people in a new, more intimate way than he has before. It has nothing to do with the denial or subjugation of Jesus' personal authority or the authority of his teaching. That is not why he was going away.

The second, which appears to be a conflation of Luke 24:5 and Matthew 28:7, concerns the literal resurrection

of Jesus from the tomb in Jerusalem and his literal journey
to Galilee. There is no hint that the angels are cautioning
the disciples no longer to regard the Jesus of history as
their authority. Quite the opposite. In this passage the historical Jesus has become the risen Lord.

Watts's use of the third text is especially disconcerting,
for Watts, trained as an Episcopal priest and thus responsible for at least playing fair with Scripture, has seemingly
turned the meaning of the original on its head. The text
as quoted is only the first half of John 5:39 in which Jesus
is addressing the religious authorities.

Here is the remainder of the verse and the one following:
"You search the scriptures, because you think that in them
you have eternal life; and it is they that bear witness to me;
yet you refuse to come to me that you may have life." In
other words, Jesus is not accusing his listeners of giving
the historical record, the Scriptures, too much credence but
too little attention. The Old Testament witnesses to who
Jesus is, but these "religious" Jews have missed the meaning of that witness. In other words, this text when placed
in context actually works against Watts's contention. It proclaims the historical Jesus as the source of life.

We conclude this section, therefore, by reiterating the
principle of responsible reading which has throughout
these passages been ignored: the text of Scripture should
first be understood within the context in which it occurs.
Any reading which contradicts the meaning of the text in
context cannot be a proper interpretation.

Misreading No. 5: Collapsing Contexts
When two or more unrelated texts are treated as if they
belonged together, we have the fallacy of collapsing contexts. This reading error can be especially knotty because
it is the corruption of a perfectly good principle of reading: to compare Scripture with Scripture. We are respon-

sible as good readers of the Bible to make use of every text bearing on the subject we wish to understand. To select some texts which agree with our preconceived ideas and ignore those that don't is, in fact, a major mistake (see Misreading No. 11, *selective citing*, pp. 80-82). But it is equally possible to put texts together which don't belong together. This, too, can produce confusion. We will look at one major example.

Consider the biblical documentation given by the Mormons for their belief in the existence of each human being prior to physical conception. "We all lived in a premortal existence, as spirits, with our Father in Heaven," says the Mormon missionary manual.[6] There is no question that this idea is taught in the *Doctrine and Covenants* (93:23, 29), the *Pearl of Great Price* (Moses 3:5; Abraham 3:22-23), and perhaps in the Book of Mormon, though the reference given in the manual to Alma 13:3 does not necessarily imply the premortal existence of the human soul.[7] But there is every reason to deny that the Bible itself contains this doctrine.

To document their belief, the Mormons bring together a number of biblical texts that turn out on examination not to belong together. A study of the missionary manual shows that the biblical references given for this doctrine are of three types:

1. Those verses referring to people in general but which do not specifically support the existence of human souls before conception: Jeremiah 1:5, Acts 17:26-29 and Hebrews 12:9.

Jeremiah 1:5 is the opening sentence of God's call to Jeremiah to be a prophet: "Before I formed thee in the belly I knew thee; and before thou camest forth out of the womb I sanctified thee, and I ordained thee a prophet unto the nations" (KJV). The main function of these words is to declare to Jeremiah that he is important to God, that God has a plan for his life, something Jeremiah alone is called to do. It says nothing at all about the premortal existence of Jeremiah's soul, only that God knew that Jeremiah would be his special servant. While this verse is consistent with the Mormon notion of the premortal existence of the soul, so is the standard Christian view—that what is indicated here is God's divine foreknowledge, his clear perception of what will take place in the future and his clear plan for providing for his people.

Acts 17:26-29 comes from Paul's sermon to the Greek intellectuals in Athens. It declares that God has made all nations of "one blood" and has set beforehand the "bounds of their habitation" (KJV). We are God's offspring, Paul goes on to say. None of this, of course, requires the doctrine of the premortal existence of each human spirit. Rather this passage teaches creation and providence.

Hebrews 12:9 refers to God as the "Father of spirits," thus teaching, according to the Mormons, that God gives birth to spirit children who later are given mortal bodies. However, the author of Hebrews is only saying that God is the creator, not the procreator, of all spirits, and there is no necessary connection between these "spirits" and premortal human beings. The text says nothing about when these spirits were brought into being. The Mormon interpretation is in this case a clear illustration of *overspecification* (Misreading No. 6), as we will see in the following section. The text by no means requires the doctrine of the premortal existence of human beings.

The key word here is *requires*. Often one finds in cult literature that when verses are quoted in support of some unique doctrine, those verses permit the unique doctrine but do not *require* that doctrine to explain their meaning. In fact, other verses in Scripture often explicitly deny the unique doctrine.

2. Those verses referring to Jesus Christ and no other

human being but which clearly teach or imply his pre-existence: John 1:2, 14; 8:56-58; 16:27-30; 17:3-5; Hebrews 5:8-9. Here Mormons read the Scripture in the same manner as traditional Christians, and so there is no need for analysis.

3. Those verses referring to the existence of angels before the temptation of Adam and Eve: Revelation 12:7-9. Again traditional Christians do not deny the existence of angels prior to the creation of mankind.

Now we are able to see clearly the fallacy of *collapsing contexts*. Texts which teach the pre-existence of Jesus Christ are laid side by side with texts that speak of human existence but which do not teach that doctrine. Or, in other words, texts which teach the notion that Jesus was pre-existent are used to prove that people in general existed before their earthly birth.

To the Mormons, of course, this interpretation of Scripture is legitimate because it falls neatly into their preconceived pattern of theology, their own world view. Jesus Christ was only what we ourselves can one day be. He merely preceded us in the process of evolutionary development. In fact, even God the Father was a man; and he, too, evolved. As Joseph Smith wrote, "God himself was once as we are now, and is an exalted Man and sits enthroned in yonder heavens."[8] Needless to say, the Mormon's biblical documentation for this notion is as problematic as their documentation for the notion of premortal existence.[9]

It is clear, however, that the principle of misreading behind collapsing contexts is the same one we have encountered before and will encounter again—world-view confusion. But we must put off our detailed treatment of this till chapter nine.

To avoid collapsing the contexts of the texts we are studying is sometimes difficult. The principle is to see each text first in its own immediate and then larger contexts;

if these contexts overlap with the contexts of other texts, these other texts may be relevant. That is, if two or more texts talk about the same subject in a similar way, then when we study them together we are not collapsing the contexts. But even as we put them together, we want to keep in mind their original contexts.

Misreading No. 6: Overspecification

As human beings we tend to be curious—sometimes over-curious, longing to know what we do not know, to go a step beyond the ordinary person in insight and knowledge. In science this curiosity leads to new hypotheses, new experiments—sometimes down blind alleys and sometimes to new knowledge. In business it leads to speculation and hence sometimes to financial success and sometimes to bankruptcy. In religion it leads to study, to speculative theology and sometimes to new spiritual insight and sometimes to answers to our questions beyond what can yet be truly known through Scripture.

Curiosity has led Archie Matson, for example, to seek in occult philosophy answers to questions which are only sketchily addressed by the Bible. Matson writes, "Mediumship spells out in much greater detail and perhaps accuracy a picture of the waiting world [the realm beyond death] to which our earlier chapters on the Bible, science, deathbed scenes, apparitions and Lazarus's experience only point in a partial and shadowy way. . . . Mediumship is the crown which gives clarity to all the rest. None of them, not even the Bible, could carry the conviction to the modern mind standing by itself."[10] We will consider later the thrust toward new sources of revelation triggered by overweening curiosity (see pp. 115-18 on Misreading No. 18). Here we are concerned with what happens to our reading of Scripture when we draw from a text a more detailed or *specific* conclusion than is legitimate.

Case 1. One of the texts used by the Mormons to document premortal existence is a case in point. I have quoted it above (p. 59) but will do so again: "Before I formed thee [Jeremiah] in the belly I knew thee; and before thou camest forth out of the womb I sanctified thee, and I ordained thee a prophet unto the nations" (Jer. 1:5).

The Mormons say, "Don't you see? Jeremiah existed before he was in the womb, before he was conceived. That is, he was a 'spirit child,' one of the 'intelligences' whom God foreknew and thus appointed to be a prophet. And," they would continue, "it's just like we are taught in the *Pearl of Great Price* (Abraham 3:22-23): 'Now the Lord had shown unto me, Abraham, the intelligences that were organized before the world was; and among all these there were many of the noble and great ones; And God saw that these souls were good, and he stood in the midst of them, and he said: These I will make my rulers....' " So by comparing one Mormon scripture (the Bible) with another Mormon scripture *(Pearl of Great Price)* Mormons conclude that Jeremiah 1:5 refers to the premortal existence of people.

But if the *Pearl of Great Price* is not authoritative—and for Christians it isn't—then this is clearly to overspecify the meaning of Jeremiah 1:5. To be sure, the Mormon reading is *consistent* with this text as such, but it is not *required* by the text. And, as we have seen above, even the Mormons can seem to find few other verses which even allow as a *possible* meaning the notion of the premortal existence of ordinary men and women.

Case 2. In her *Key to the Scriptures* Mary Baker Eddy, founder of Christian Science, comments on Genesis 1:1 ("In the beginning God created the heaven and the earth" KJV):

The infinite has no beginning. This word *beginning* is employed to signify *the only*—that is, the eternal verity and unity of God and man, including the universe. The creative Principle—Life, Truth, and Love—is God. The universe reflects God. There is but one creator and one creation. This creation consists of the unfolding of spiritual ideas and their identities, which are embraced in the infinite Mind and forever reflected. These ideas range from the infinitesimal to infinity, and the highest ideas are the sons and daughters of God.[11]

Traditional Christians may find some of her comments acceptable. "The universe reflects God," for example, suggests Psalm 19:1. But most of her commentary goes well beyond anything covered in Genesis 1:1. This passage also illustrates other reading errors; for us now, however, it stands as a clear example of overspecification.

Misreading the Bible in this way is a constant temptation for all of us. Somehow we want *the Bible* to say just what *we* want the Bible to say, and so we read into it a meaning that is either not possible at all or is far more specific than the text actually confirms. In reading and interpreting Scripture we should strive to draw from any given text only so much as is specified by that text taken in context and from any given set of texts only so much as they specify when seen first in their immediate contexts and then in the larger framework of scriptural thought.

Of course, when we move from the "meaning" of any Scripture to its "application" in our lives, we will necessarily make the text specific to us. Its significance will vary from person to person. This application, however, must never be read back into the text such that every other reader would be required to hold this application as the meaning of the text itself.

Misreading No. 7: Word Play
The Bible must be recognized as a work of literature in its native tongue as well as in translation. If we are to do a

word study, that is, examine the etymology (word origin), definitions, use of the word in various biblical texts and so forth, we must work from the Greek or Hebrew. Some study can be accomplished by use of an English-language concordance, but it must be checked against the words in the original. Some full concordances like *Strong's Exhaustive Concordance of the Bible* allow those without knowledge of the original languages a fair degree of help, certainly enough to avoid the following error. One commentary starts off on a promising note: "The word *Adam* is from the Hebrew *adamah,* signifying *the red color of the ground, dust, nothingness."* It looks like the writer is going to play fair. Hebrew would appear to be the basis for the comment.[12] Then come the following remarks:

> Divide the name Adam into two syllables, and it reads *a dam,* or obstruction. This suggests the thought of something fluid, of mortal mind in solution. It further suggests the thought of that "darkness . . . upon the face of the deep," when matter or dust was deemed the agent of Deity in creating man,—when matter, as that which is accursed, stood opposed to Spirit. Here *a dam* is not a mere play upon words; it stands for obstruction, error, even the supposed separation of man from God, and the obstacle which the serpent, sin, would impose between man and his creator.[13]

Suddenly the writer has turned from the Hebrew to the English and developed an exegesis based on a pun. This is such an obvious misreading that I might not have used this passage as an example had it not derived from a major text from a major cult. What is the source? Mary Baker Eddy's *Science and Health with Key to the Scriptures.*

Avoiding this misreading should not be difficult. Whenever you get the urge to play on a word in the English version of the Bible, don't yield to it. Treasure it in your heart as a joke like the one that claims that the patriarch

Joseph played tennis because he "served in Pharaoh's court." That's all the status it deserves.

Misreading No. 8: The Figurative Fallacy

The *figurative fallacy* is far more difficult to avoid than word play. Every reader must determine the way language is being used. Does the fact that in John 4 the word *water* is used both literally and figuratively mean it is always used this way in Scripture? And is the figurative meaning always the same? If a word has a literal reference as a part of an historical narrative, does that mean it does not have a figurative meaning? Or vice versa, if a word is used figuratively, must it also signify something literal?

Most Bible scholars would, I think, answer no to all of the above. Nonetheless, that does not help us as readers to determine when a particular word or sentence is being used solely in a literal way, solely in a figurative way or in a combination of ways. As readers we must learn to develop good judgment. Examining some errors that have been made by the cults will help us get a perspective on our task. We will first look at those misreadings that involve *mistaking literal language for figurative language.*

Case 1. Mary Baker Eddy turns the figurative fallacy into a principle when she writes, "In Christian Science we learn that the substitution of the spiritual for the material definition of a Scriptural word often elucidates the meaning of the inspired writer. On this account this chapter ["Glossary"] is added. It contains the metaphysical interpretation of Bible terms, giving their spiritual sense, which is also their original meaning."[14]

In the glossary that follows 125 words are given their figurative, that is for Eddy, their actual meaning. *Dove,* for example, is "a symbol of divine Science; purity and peace; hope and faith."[15] *Evening* is "mistiness of mortal thought; weariness of mortal mind; obscured views; peace and rest."[16] *Morning* is "light; symbol of Truth; revelation and progress."[17]

Most of the words in the glossary are defined without reference to any specific text of Scripture. Under the word *day*, however, we find this: "The irradiance of Life; light the spiritual idea of Truth and Love. 'And the evening and the morning were the first day.' (Genesis i.5) The objects of time and sense disappear in the illumination of spiritual understanding, and Mind measures time according to the good that is unfolded. This unfolding is God's day, and 'there shall be no night there.' "[18] The second quotation, though not documented, is from Revelation 21:25 and refers in context to the city of God. Regardless of how we examine the full contexts of these words—*morning, evening, day*—there is no way we can arrive at Eddy's "spiritual" meaning. Unless we accept her as a special prophet and *Science and Health with Key to the Scriptures* as new revelation, there is no reason to use her glossary as a guide.

As traditional Christians we must simply conclude that Eddy has committed the figurative fallacy; she has mistaken the literal for the figurative. It is interesting to note that this particular fallacy is a natural outgrowth of Christian Science theology. In Eddy's world view, only spirit exists; matter does not exist except as an error in our human perception. So any word signifying something material on a literal level is either a label for error or a metaphor for truth. *Adam*, for example, is "error, a falsity; the belief in 'original sin,' sickness and death. . . ."[19]

As we will see in chapter eight, Eddy is not the only modern prophet to propose an ornate spiritual (figurative) meaning to biblical terms. Emanuel Swedenborg, from whom the Church of the New Jerusalem derives, likewise developed such an approach to Bible reading. (See the discussion of both Eddy and Swedenborg below, pp. 109-15.) It is, in fact, the constant temptation of readers who somehow believe there must be more to the Bible than meets the eye of steady reason. Hidden in the literal is the figurative, the real, the spiritual meaning, and we must find the key. The cults are filled with "keys," but when each key is used to unlock the text, the meaning that emerges is unique and fails to square with other meanings unlocked by other keys.

Traditional Bible scholars use a different principle: where the Bible itself suggests that words or narratives are being used symbolically, we should follow the suggestions of the Bible; where the Bible is silent on such symbolism, we should stick with the plain, straightforward sense of the text; in no case will a symbolic or figurative reading contradict any biblical teaching which derives from texts which are obviously intended to be taken in their plain ordinary sense. We must not, for example, interpret a parable of Jesus so as to conflict with Paul's letter to the Romans or use an event in the life of Abraham to typify an idea which Jesus calls into question. This will not solve all problems of figurative language, but it will dramatically reduce the number of difficult texts.

There is, however, another side to the figurative fallacy. One can also *mistake the figurative for the literal.*

Case 2. In his theology of the Mormon faith Talmage considers what he believes is Old Testament prophecy regarding the Book of Mormon. The text to which Talmage refers is Isaiah 29:1-6:

> Woe to Ariel, to Ariel, the city where David dwelt! add ye year to year; let them kill sacrifices. Yet I will distress Ariel, and there shall be heaviness and sorrow: and it shall be unto me as Ariel. And I will camp against thee round about, and will lay siege against thee with a mount, and I will raise forts against thee. And thou shalt be brought down, and shalt speak out of the ground, and thy speech shall be low out of the dust, and thy voice shall be, as of one that hath a familiar spirit, out of the ground,

and thy speech shall whisper out of the dust. Moreover
the multitude of thy strangers shall be like small dust,
and the multitude of the terrible ones shall be as chaff
that passeth away: yea, it shall be at an instant suddenly.
Thou shalt be visited of the LORD of hosts with thunder,
and with earthquake, and great noise, with storm and
tempest, and the flame of devouring fire. (KJV)

The phrase which Talmage wants to pick up as prophesy-
ing the Book of Mormon is this: "Thy speech shall be low
out of the dust, and thy voice shall be, as of one that hath a
familiar spirit, out of the ground, and thy speech shall
whisper out of the dust" (v. 4). To do this, of course, he
must first show that the "voice" is not Ariel (that is, Jerusalem, the city of David, v. 1) but someone else. Talmage
quotes Orson Pratt, an earlier "latter-day apostle" to this
effect: "These predictions of Isaiah could not refer to
Ariel of Jerusalem, because their speech has not been 'out
of the ground,' or 'low out of the dust'; but it refers to the
remnant of Joseph who were destroyed in America up-
wards of fourteen hundred years ago. The Book of Mormon describes their downfall, and truly it was great and
terrible. . . . This remnant of Joseph in their distress became *as* Ariel."[20]

Why does Pratt conclude that Jerusalem's voice was
never "out of the ground"? What does "out of the ground"
mean? Could it not refer to almost any expression of grief
that followed Jerusalem's destruction? The Lamentations
of Jeremiah, for example, would do quite well.

Moreover, many nations have been destroyed, laid bare.
Poland was "*as* Ariel" in World War 2. And Jerzy Kosinski's
novel *The Painted Bird* is a voice "out of the ground."

But there are also other reasons to question Pratt's reading. "It shall be unto me as Ariel" almost certainly does not
refer to a second people but is a further allusion to Jerusalem. The word *Ariel* itself as it appears in Ezekiel 43:15-16

means "altar." The phrase, "as Ariel," might thus be rendered "and it shall be unto me as an altar, that is, as in a sacrifice." Jerusalem will be placed, as it were, on an altar and burnt. Either of the two major destructions of Jerusalem in 587 B.C. or A.D. 70 would fit as fulfillment.

The real reason for working so hard to show that this passage does not refer to Jerusalem comes in Talmage's next point: "Isaiah's prediction that the nation thus brought down should 'speak out of the ground,' with speech 'low out of the dust' was literally fulfilled in the bringing forth of the Book of Mormon, the original of which was taken out of the ground, and the voice of the record is as that of one speaking from the dust."[21] I would suggest that Talmage and Pratt before him have mistaken the figurative for the literal. Clearly, unless there are other good reasons for thinking the Book of Mormon is the word of God, we may take his literal reading of the figurative as rather fanciful.

The important point in all this to remember is that as responsible Bible readers we must understand the text in the manner in which it was written. It will not always be easy to tell just what any given phrase, like "out of the ground," was intended to mean. On some matters we may have to withhold judgment. But when we see a reading like the Mormons give Isaiah 29:1-6, we may well wish to do more than doubt it. Other possible interpretations—which we ourselves can discern—are far more likely.

**Misreading No. 9: Speculative Readings
of Predictive Prophecy**
There is nothing in Scripture more difficult to treat with certainty than the interpretation of predictive prophecy, especially those prophecies in both the Old and New Testaments which were not fulfilled by the time of the New Testament era and interpreted as such by New Testament

authors. Yet it is just such prophecy that is emphasized by many of the cults who base their authority at least partially on the Bible. The Jehovah's Witnesses, for example, have an elaborate and unique interpretation of prophecy.

We cannot hope to deal with this particular problem in depth in this book. Christians themselves disagree markedly on specific meanings of specific passages. Generally, however, traditional Christians hold the central doctrines of the Christian faith in common and do not allow their divergent understandings of prophetic passages to delineate for them the central character of their faith. I will not, therefore, presume to untangle the knots of disagreement among Christians. We will, rather, look at one example of interpreting prophecy which goes beyond any acceptable limits. We have already seen one case of this in our discussion of the figurative fallacy (pp. 68-70). We will draw another from the same religious group.

Concerning Ezekiel 37:15-23, Talmage comments,

Ezekiel saw in vision the coming together of the stick of Judah, and the stick of Joseph, signifying the Bible and the Book of Mormon. The passage last referred to reads, in the words of Ezekiel: "The word of the Lord came again unto me, saying, Moreover, thou son of man, take thee one stick, and write upon it, For Judah, and for the children of Israel his companions: then take another stick, and write upon it, For Joseph, the stick of Ephraim, and for all the house of Israel his companions: And join them one to another into one stick; and they shall become one in thine hand."

When we call to mind the ancient custom in the making of books—that of writing on long strips of parchment and rolling the same on rods or sticks, the use of the word "stick" as equivalent to "book" in the passage becomes apparent. At the time of this utterance, the Israelites had divided into two nations known as the

kingdom of Judah and that of Israel, or Ephraim. Plainly
the separate records of Judah and Joseph are here
referred to. Now, as we have seen, the Nephite nation
comprised the descendents of Lehi who belonged to the
tribe of Manasseh, of Ishmael who was an Ephraimite,
and of Zoram whose tribal relation is not definitely
stated. The Nephites were then of the tribes of Joseph;
and their record or "stick" is as truly represented by the
Book of Mormon as is the "stick" of Judah by the Bible.[22]
Plainly the separate records of Judah (the Bible) and
Joseph (Book of Mormon) are here referred to? Only, I
would suggest, if one is already committed to the Book of
Mormon as the word of God and only if the story of the
Nephites as told by the Book of Mormon actually hap-
pened.[23]

On a purely literary basis, however, an important reading is in question. What are the two sticks to which the
passage refers? They are indeed used in a figurative way,
for two names are to be inscribed upon them. But are they
a figure for books or for something else?

The text says that each stick was to be inscribed—one
"Judah" or "for Judah," the other "Joseph" or "for Joseph."
Anything relating to those two names could be meant. Since
both are names of tribes of Israel, why go beyond the immediate possibilities that present themselves—matters relating to the Jewish nation of Ezekiel's day and after? The
Nephites are supposed to be descendents of Joseph, but
only in the Book of Mormon. The Bible itself knows nothing of them.

Though undoubtedly there are other ways to understand the prophecy, let me simply quote John B. Taylor's
commentary on this passage. As you read what Taylor
says, ask yourself, which is a more likely understanding of
the text: Taylor's or Talmage's? Note, too, that Taylor
recognizes the tentative nature of his own interpretation.

Once again the prophet speaks his word with the aid of a symbolical action (cf. 4:1; 5:1). He is told by the Lord to make two sticks (lit. "pieces of wood") and to mark them with the words, *For Judah and For Joseph*. These represent the two kingdoms of former days, before Samaria fell to the Assyrians under Sargon II (722/1 BC) and Israel, the northern kingdom, lost her identity. He is to take one of them in his right hand, concealing one end of it in his clenched fist. Then he is to take the other stick and join it to the first one, end to end. His clenched fist will thus grasp the place where the two sticks meet, and it will appear as if he is holding one long stick in the middle. Understood in this way, it is not necessary to postulate any kind of miracle in the symbolic act. The meaning of the action is that in the restored Israel, the old divisions of north and south will be abolished and the nation will be united in God's hand. The interpretation of this, however, raises a number of controversial issues. If the inhabitants of Israel/Samaria were scattered throughout the Assyrian Empire, is there any prospect of their descendants being literally brought back, with the exiles from Judah, into the promised land? Or are we to understand "Israel" as consisting simply of those men of northern tribal origin who had associated themselves with Judah from time to time? Do we allegorize it all and see it simply as a picture of the church, the new Israel, united in the future kingdom of God? The problems become particularly acute, when the reader approaches this passage with the question foremost in his mind: "Has this prophecy been fulfilled?" The fulfilment of prophecy is a question which must always take second place after the issue of correct exegesis has been settled.[24]

In the analysis which follows this, Taylor goes on to give a tentative answer to the question of the prophecy's fulfillment. But in none of his lengthy discussion does Taylor once refer to the possibility that the two sticks could mean two books. Why? Because there is a more natural explanation suggested by the text itself and the context of Jewish history.

This single example will suffice to show the character of cultic use of prophecy. The principle of good reading we want to raise as a result is simply this: when the New Testament declares an Old Testament prophecy to be fulfilled, do not look for another fulfillment; when any prophecy does not appear to be fulfilled, measure all modern attempts to identify its fulfillment against the backdrop of the rest of the Bible. And refuse to accept any interpretation which serves to substantiate a religious philosophy that is nonbiblical in other more obvious ways.

The Natural Literary Guards
Because the Bible is to be read as ordinary literature, there are a host of guards against misinterpretation. A text of Scripture can't mean just anything anyone wants it to. It is not true that you can prove anything from the Bible—not if you recognize its character as literature. As literature, the Bible is subject to the guard of immediate and larger contexts and of genre (poetry, chronicle, parable, epistle, etc.).

The more we recognize these guards against error and use them in our own Bible reading, the more we will recognize when they are violated by cult writers and evangelists. Experience with reading literature of any kind is itself excellent training for reading the Bible correctly.

Chapter 6
Scripture as Evidence

The Bible does not come to us automatically bearing its own interpretation. It does not impress its meaning immediately on each reader's mind such that all of us receive the same message. Good Bible reading requires good thinking.[1]

This and the following chapter concentrate on misreadings deriving from errors in thinking, errors in logic. The present chapter focuses on mistakes made in *inductive reasoning*, that is, reasoning which begins with data, facts, evidence of various kinds, and then draws general conclusions. We observe, for example, that most people die when they approach about eighty or ninety years or so, and that none of them seem to survive much past a hundred years. So, we say, all people are mortal. Or we have never seen a rock suspend itself in midair. So, we say, rocks fall if

not supported. Not all conclusions to inductive reasoning
are that easy to make or that certain to be true. But these
ideal examples show the process.

The Scripture, like falling rocks and dying people, also
supplies data—information from which conclusions can
and should be drawn. We are to search the Scriptures daily
to see if those things we are hearing and learning from the
various spiritual teachers are true (Acts 17:11).

Jesus himself relied on inductive reasoning. John the
Baptist once sent two of his disciples to Jesus to ask, "Are
you he who is to come [that is, the Messiah], or shall we look
for another?" How did Jesus respond? "In that hour he
cured many of diseases and plagues and evil spirits, and on
many that were blind he bestowed sight. And he [Jesus]
answered them, 'Go and tell John what you have seen and
heard: the blind receive their sight, the lame walk, lepers
are cleansed, and the deaf hear, the dead are raised up, the
poor have good news preached to them. And blessed is he
who takes no offense at me' " (Lk. 7:21-23).

What Jesus did and said was just what was prophesied of
the Messiah in, for example, Isaiah 29:18-19; 35:5-6. The
point is: When all the data stack up in favor of a proposition, one should presume the proposition true. If there is
counterdata, one should examine it to see if it really does
weigh against the proposition. If so, something is probably
wrong with the proposition itself. We may then wish to try
again to formulate a view which really fits the facts—all the
facts we not only have easily at hand but can get at hand by
research.

We will look now at three misreadings which fail to use
inductive reasoning properly.

Misreading No. 10: Saying but Not Citing
The first task of anyone who wishes to make a case based on
data is to place the data into evidence. When we try to make

a case from Scripture, for example, we often hear the rejoinder, "But the Bible is full of contradictions." Usually when one asks for an example, the respondent is at a loss, or he gives an example which will not stand up under even the most cursory analysis. In any case, the proponent of any position must show us his facts. Jesus did not just tell John's disciples what he had been doing; he showed them. Sometimes, however, cult writers do not do this. They proclaim that there is evidence, but they don't show us.

Case 1. Two scientifically minded writers who say but do not always cite may conveniently be considered together. Both accept the same principle of biblical interpretation and make a similar case for similar conclusions. As Irwin Ginsburgh says, "The words used in the Book of Genesis represent the best thinking and understanding of its compilers. For instance, their explanation of a modern scientific idea would be obscure to us since they did not have our technical language upon which to draw. If twentieth century technical synonyms are substituted for some of the general words in the Book of Genesis, it becomes possible to understand some of the obscure passages in this fundamental work in terms of modern day science."[2]

Both science and the Bible, Ginsburgh argues, place the origin of man about six thousand years ago.[3] And, after comparing a few phrases from Genesis 1 with modern science he concludes, "They both could be describing the same events."[4] The tree of knowledge, for example, "could, in modern language, be translated as being a central computer, since knowledge is the important concept rather than the tree."[5]

Suddenly we are brought up short. What is a computer doing in the Garden of Eden? Ginsburgh explains: "Here I make the one major assumption of my concept—and that is, the Garden of Eden was a space ship that crash-landed on Earth, and that it carried two superior space people, Adam and Eve."[6] Obviously we have here a case of *world-view confusion* (Misreading No. 20). But we will not pause to comment on that. Our point is that after a long build-up and with very few references to the Bible (and all of those almost as strained as the tree equaling a computer), Ginsburgh comments: "I am certain there is other evidence that can be found in the Bible, if we knew how to look for it."[7] But this is saying, not citing. If there is, show us. If not, don't pretend there is.

Case 2. Another researcher into things past who treats the Bible in a similar fashion is Erich von Däniken. He argues, for example, that the ark of the covenant was a radio "transmitter" linking Moses and a space ship, one of the "chariots of the Gods." But let us focus only on his casual attempt to document one part of his case. "Without actually consulting Exodus," he writes, "I seem to remember that the Ark was often surrounded by flashing sparks. . . ." Alluding to "flashing sparks," of course, serves to count in favor of seeing the ark as a transmitter.[8]

But von Däniken's description looked strange to me. So I did actually consult Exodus. Nowhere is it said to be surrounded by flashing sparks or fire or anything similar. A thorough examination of the Old Testament references to the ark produced only five that could remotely suggest "flashing sparks." In Leviticus 10:1-3, the sons of Aaron took their censors and "offered unholy fire before the LORD." For this sacrilege "fire came forth from the presence of the LORD and devoured them." This happened in the tabernacle and thus somewhere near the ark (cf. Lev. 16:2). In 2 Samuel 6:6-7 (parallel passage, 1 Chron. 13:9-10) God "smote" Uzzah because he placed his hand on the ark to steady it as it was being moved. But no sparks or fire are mentioned. In 1 Chronicles 16:1-2 burnt offerings are offered near the ark. But nothing like flashing sparks appear. None of the other Old Testament references to the

ark (and there are a great many) have even as much relevance as the ones mentioned.

The text most fitting von Däniken's is Revelation 11:19:
"Then God's temple in heaven was opened, and the ark of
his covenant was seen within his temple; and there were
flashes of lightning, voices, peals of thunder, an earthquake, and heavy hail." But here the ark is in heaven. And
the time, if the scene is understood as set in time at all, is the
future. Even the lightning may not be "close" to the ark in
the temple, for it is associated with an earthquake and hail
which seem more likely to refer to happenings on earth.
Morever, in Revelation we are dealing with a vision. To
treat the vision as if it were history or flat description of
future or past events is to fail to see the text in its literary
context.

There would, of course, be no need to make any of these
rejoinders to von Däniken if he had not assumed—like
Ginsburgh—that the plain, nontechnical language of the
Bible conceals descriptions of either scientific concepts or
advanced technological artifacts. The problem is the assumption: it encourages the most fanciful of interpretations of ancient texts. In the case before us it even encourages the fabrication of evidence—saying but not citing.

Case 3. In a very different situation, the English Buddhist scholar, Christmas Humphreys, commits the same
fallacy. Humphreys has just explained the Buddhist
idea that "there is nothing in man which entitles him to
say, 'I am this and you are that', through all eternity."[9]
That is, he has presented the idea that all is one (Atman
is Brahman), a distinctively pantheistic idea. Then he
says, "Above the clamour of competative strife the self-
same Teaching of Christ remains unheard."[10] But where
does Christ teach this? We are not told. A Christian can,
however, counter with texts which teach the opposite:
Genesis 1:26-27 (which Jesus quoted in Mt. 19:4-6); John

14:2 (if we are not distinct as individuals, why will heaven need so many "rooms" to accommodate us?). A general respect for individuals is part of the entire Judeo-Christian world view and one of the chief characteristics distinguishing it from Buddhism.[11]

Evidence which is said to exist but not shown to exist is not sufficient for any inductive argument. If someone would have us believe that the Bible teaches any particular doctrine—either orthodox or eccentric—we must ask them, first, to quote "chapter and verse" and, second, to explain why these Scriptures taken in context are relevant to the issue. Apart from this, we would be well to remain skeptical and unconvinced.

Misreading No. 11: Selective Citing
Another misuse of evidence in argument comes when only a portion of the relevant texts is cited. You can "prove" almost anything from the Bible if you are allowed to select verses or portions of verses as if they told the whole story.

The Jehovah's Witnesses believe that, while Jesus existed in heaven before he was born on earth, he was, nonetheless, a created being. "This child, Jesus, was not God, but God's son," says the Jehovah's Witnesses book *The Truth That Leads to Eternal Life*.[12] This teaching is, of course, a direct contradiction of the doctrine of the Trinity—that God is triune, Father, Son and Holy Spirit. As the Athanasian Creed says, "The Father is God, the Son is God, and the Holy Spirit is God, and yet there are not three Gods, but one God."

"Let God Be True," another Witness publication, devotes a chapter to the question "Is there a Trinity?" and answers it in the negative, but it does so primarily by selectively citing and commenting on the verses which orthodox Christians use to substantiate the doctrine. The Witnesses claim that traditional Christians base the Trinity on a misunderstanding of the following texts: 1 John 5:7; 1 Timothy 3:16; John

1:1; and John 10:30.

The Witnesses correctly point out that the most reliable Greek texts do not include the specifically Trinitarian phrases of 1 John 5:7. But as Hoekema says, "No reputable theologian from any evangelical denomination would use this passage today as a proof-text for the Trinity!"[13] Hoekema also concedes that 1 Timothy 3:16 is more correctly translated as the Witnesses claim and thus Christians do not base their case on the earlier reading Witnesses are attacking.[14] The Witnesses refute the clear declaration that "the Word was God" in John 1:1 by retranslating it "the Word was a god." But both Anthony Hoekema and Bruce Metzger show how their translation is illegitimate, a twisted translation (Misreading No. 2).[15] (I take up the Witnesses' translation of John 1:1 in detail below [pp. 139-40 and 161-63]). Finally, the Witnesses interpret John 10:30 ("I and the Father are one") as referring only to their unity in "agreement, purpose and organization."[16] But, as Hoekema and Metzger ask, Why, then, did the Jews try to stone Jesus? Obviously, they thought he was claiming deity (Jn. 10:33). The context shows the Witnesses' interpretation of Jesus' words to be wide of the mark.

But more is at stake here than what the Jehovah's Witnesses say. What they do not say may be just as important, for they completely ignore many other passages which give evidence in favor of the deity of Christ and doctrine of the Trinity: Matthew 28:19; John 20:28; 1 Corinthians 6:11 and 12:4-5; 2 Corinthians 1:21-22 and 13:14; Galatians 3: 11-14; 1 Thessalonians 5:18-19 and 1 Peter 1:1-2.[17]

Metzger furthermore shows that the New Testament applies "to Jesus Christ passages from the Old Testament which refer to Jehovah."[18] For example, Isaiah 6:1, 3, 10 records the prophet's vision of Jehovah. But John 12:37-41 says that what Isaiah saw was the glory of Jesus Christ, thus equating Christ and Jehovah. This connection is clear even in the Witnesses' own New World Translation.

Another of Metzger's illustrations, however, has been obscured by the NWT. Using the American Standard Version (1901) which was, prior to the NWT, the Witnesses' standard for study, Metzger shows how Isaiah 60:19 ("Jehovah will be unto thee an everlasting light, and thy God thy glory") is applied to Jesus by the Gospel of Luke 2:32 ("A light for revelation to the Gentiles, and the glory of thy people Israel"). The NWT, however, translates Isaiah 60: 19 as "And Jehovah must become to you an infinitely lasting light, and your God your beauty" and Luke 2:32 as "a light for removing the veil from the nations and a glory of your people Israel." The application to Jesus of words about Jehovah is thus obscured.

Whether the Witnesses acknowledge it or not, the Trinitarian pattern was deeply impressed upon the mind of the apostles and the early church. The formal expression of the doctrine did not come until later in church history when some Christian teachers were espousing what others took to be heresy. But the New Testament writers fell with ease into the pattern of linking the Father, the Son and the Holy Spirit (as the above verses attest). To object, as the Jehovah's Witnesses do, that the word *Trinity* itself is not found in Scripture is off the mark. That argument works against the Witnesses as well, for, as Metzger points out, one of their favorite words, *theocracy,* is not found in the Bible either.[19] The point is not whether the word is there but whether the concept is there. By the selective citing of Scripture they have not considered all the relevant lines of evidence.

Misreading No. 12: Inadequate Evidence
Some parts of the Bible are obscure, puzzling to say the least. Scholars simply don't know what is being said or referred to. Sometimes even when we have considered all the evidence seemingly available in Scripture there is not

enough to satisfy our curiosity or to draw solid conclusions. The Scripture does not answer every question we
bring to it, though only by asking and seeking are we likely
to discover just which questions can't be answered.

The inadequacy of scriptural data, however, has not kept
people from speculating. Oftentimes, then, seeing how
their speculation matches other evidence or other speculation, the speculators conclude their speculation is true.

Case 1. Erich von Däniken in his chapter, "Was God an
Astronaut?" takes a few obscure and puzzling passages
from Scripture and suggests how his own theory removes
the obscurity. Here von Däniken quotes from Genesis and
comments:

> "There were giants on the earth in those days; and also
> after that, when the sons of God came in unto the daugh-
> ters of men, and they bore children to them, the same
> became mighty men which were of old, men of renown"
> (Genesis 6:4).
>
> Once again we have sons of God, who interbred with
> human beings [von Däniken has just spoken about Gen.
> 6:1-2 which mentions this]. Here, too, we have the first
> mention of giants. "Giants" keep cropping up in all parts
> of the globe: in mythology of East and West, in the sagas
> of Tiahuanaco and the epics of the Eskimos. "Giants"
> haunt the pages of almost all ancient books. So they must
> have existed. What sort of creatures were they, these
> "giants"? Were they our forefathers who built the gigan-
> tic buildings and effortlessly handled the monoliths, or
> were they technically skilled space travelers from another
> star?[20]

Biblical scholars do not know who or what the giants were.
The RSV, to reflect this obscurity, transliterates the word
from Hebrew—*Nephilim*. There is simply no hard evidence
to give the modern reader a handle on this text. One thing
we can say, however, is that there are other alternatives than

the two listed by von Däniken. Large men like Goliath—or Wilt Chamberlain!—would do, for example.

Von Däniken follows his brief comment on the giants by proposing similar speculations on other obscure texts and also giving "scientific" explanations for less obscure ones. The ark of the covenant was an electrically charged radio transmitter, he says (referring to Ex. 15:10, 25:40; 2 Sam. 6:2). Sodom and Gomorrah were destroyed by astronauts in a nuclear explosion (Gen. 19:1-28); Ezekiel, who said he saw "visions of God" (Ezek. 1:1) or "the appearance of the likeness of the glory of the LORD" (Ezek. 1:28), actually saw a spacecraft.[21] Speculation is piled on speculation but the evidence for it is exceptionally thin. Each passage of Scripture has to be made to mean something either *other* than it says or *more* than it says.

Case 2. Jehovah's Witnesses are well known for refusing blood transfusions when doctors prescribe them. They build their case—as with all other of their teachings—on a close reading of the Scripture. Here is how the case is put in *The Truth That Leads to Eternal Life.*[22]

First, God made plain his respect for human life and blood. Genesis 4:8-11; 9:5-6 (concerning Abel's blood "crying" out to God from the ground, and the death penalty for murder, blood for blood) are quoted. Then 1 John 3:15 is quoted, showing that hatred is murder (1 Jn. 3:11, 12 and Mt. 5:21-22 are cited, too); abortion is then rejected on the basis of Exodus 21:22-23 and Psalm 127:3.

Second, the Bible "frequently uses 'blood' to stand for 'life.' " Leviticus 17:11 is the reference here.

Third, in the Old Testament God commanded people not to eat blood (Gen. 9:3-4) and this command is binding on Christians as well, for the "governing body of the early Christian congregation wrote to the non-Jewish believers": "The Holy Spirit and we ourselves have favored adding no further burden to you, except these necessary things, to

yourselves free from things sacrificed to idols and from
blood and from things strangled and from fornication. If
you carefully keep yourselves from these things, you will
prosper. Good health to you!" (Acts 15:28-29).[23] A further reference (Deut. 12:15-16) is used to show that people
are not to eat "the flesh of an animal that has not been bled,"
nor are we to eat "any sort of blood" (Lev. 17:10), which is
taken specifically to include human blood.[24] Thus the early
church condemned the Roman practice of quaffing "with
greedy thirst the blood of criminals slain in the arena," as
Tertullian described it in his day.

So far, as traditional Christians we may feel that the Witnesses are following the teaching of Scripture fairly well.[25]
It is what follows that appears strange. Here is the argument in the words of the Jehovah's Witnesses:

What about the use to which human blood is put today?
Medical doctors, realizing the life-sustaining power of
blood, use blood transfusions freely in their treatment of
patients. Is this in harmony with God's will? Some persons may reason that getting a blood transfusion is not
actually "eating." But is it not true that when a patient is
unable to eat through his mouth, doctors often feed him
by the same method in which a blood transfusion is ad-
ministered? Examine the scriptures carefully and notice
that they tell us to *"Keep free* from blood" and to *"abstain*
from blood." (Acts 15:20, 29) What does this mean? If a
doctor were to tell you to abstain from alcohol, would that
mean simply that you should not take it through your
mouth but that you could transfuse it directly into your
veins? Of course not! So, too, "abstaining from blood"
means not taking it into our bodies at all.[26]

Let us look at this argument closely. The key issue is whether *eating, keeping free from* and *abstaining* apply to blood
transfusion. The argument that they do is based on an
analogy. If a doctor told you to "abstain from alcohol," you

would know that that meant not to take it intravenously. Of course, *you* would know because intravenous feedings are now common.

But how can the Bible—either Old or New Testament—be used to explicitly forbid something that was invented centuries later? To be sure, if a principle is involved, this can be done. "Thou shalt not kill" clearly includes "Thou shalt not put a live electrical wire in thy neighbor's bathtub." Between murder by sword and murder by guns, bombs, high-voltage wires and laser beams there is no category confusion. Murder is murder.

But a *blood transfusion* is not *eating*. A transfusion replenishes the supply of essential, life-sustaining fluid that has otherwise drained away or become incapable of performing its vital tasks in the body. A blood transfusion is not even equivalent to intravenous feeding because the blood so given does not function as food. The Jehovah's Witnesses argument is based on a false analogy.

We conclude, therefore, that the biblical evidence for their rejection of blood transfusions is not sufficient. Their own case does not end here, however. In the book we have been examining they continue to argue (1) that avoiding transfusions does not work a hardship but an advantage because of the promise in Acts 15:29 ("If you carefully keep yourselves from these things, you will prosper. Good health to you!"); (2) a transfusion does not always help; (3) even if it did help, you would be breaking God's law ("If we try to save our life, or soul, by breaking God's law, we will lose it everlastingly," as Mt. 16:25 indicates); (4) if one does die, there is always the resurrection promised by 1 Thessalonians 4:13-14; and (5) by refusing to yield to the use of blood transfusions we will "keep our eye on God's provision of *eternal* life for those who walk in the way of truth."[27]

This argument which moves in strange and surprising ways is concluded as follows:

As never before, there is an urgent need for people everywhere to get God's viewpoint of life. They need to learn of the provision that Jehovah God himself has made to save life. He sent his Son Jesus Christ to shed his own lifeblood on behalf of those who will exercise faith, and he resurrected him from the dead. (Hebrews 13:20, 21) It is not by blood transfusions but only by means of faith in Jesus' shed blood that salvation can be had. And it is urgent to gain and exercise that faith now before this old system of things comes to its end. If we have learned about this loving provision, then we should feel moved to tell others about it. Godly concern for the lives of other people will move us to do it with zeal and boldness. (Ezekiel 3:17-21) If we shoulder this responsibility and persist in it until they have all had opportunity to hear, we will be able to say, as did the apostle Paul: "I am clean from the blood of all men, for I have not held back from telling you all the counsel of God."—Acts 20:26, 27.[28]

This final paragraph of the chapter epitomizes the frustrating way the Witnesses argue from Scripture. A slightly eccentric reading of one text of Scripture is linked with another slightly eccentric reading of another text, a few noneccentric readings are added and, as a traditional Christian we find ourselves in an odd forest of trees that look a bit like elms and oaks and pines and aspen but upon examination aren't really elms and oaks and pines and aspen but vegetation belonging to another planet circling another sun.

If we look again at that final paragraph we find a number of notions with which we would like to think we agree. But then we see what the final verse must mean if we follow the thrust of the chapter. Acts 20:26-27 must mean, in paraphrase, "I am clean from the blood of all men because I have not had a blood transfusion and I have not refrained

from telling you that you ought not to have one either."
One wonders what the apostle Paul and the Ephesians to
whom he was writing would have made of that.

Argument and Evidence
We have seen in this chapter what happens when the evidence adduced in favor of a position simply is either not all
there or not there at all. The case may appear to be made.
And many an unwary reader has been convinced by such
arguments. But it ought not to be so for us.

The antidote to such arguments is not to seal ourselves
off from anything not from our own particular Christian
tradition. For one thing, that is not possible, especially
today with all manner of ideas vying for attention on television, the radio, the movies and the newspaper. Second,
that would imply that we (our tradition, our denomination,
our pastor, our fellowship group, our friends) have a corner on the truth. That is simply not true.

The antidote to these arguments is to examine them carefully, asking, What is the source (chapter and verse, please)?
Are all the relevant data there? Is it adequate? How do
traditional Christians deal with the data? The more you
know the Scripture, the more deeply you study it on your
own, the easier you will find the answers to those questions
when you need them.

Chapter 7
Reasoning from Scripture

U nderstanding Scripture, seeing each text in its context and getting an overall view of the scheme of ideas into which each text fits, involves more than simply bringing all the evidence out into the open. It involves more than drawing proper generalizations from the scriptural data.

Other matters of good reasoning also come into play. When we begin to put the texts of Scripture together and note their relationships to each other, we are beginning to think systematically about Scripture. Thus it is possible to fall into errors that have to do with *deductive reasoning*, thinking that begins with general principles and argues toward more specific ideas or application.

The commandment, "Thou shalt not steal" (Ex. 20:15 KJV), we might find ourselves arguing, means that truck drivers should not have the person who weighs their trucks

tamper with the scales to make it appear that they have
hauled more than they actually have. In this case the word
steal is a general term including all manner of specific
meanings from a trucker juggling weights to an accountant
juggling the books.

That this commandment includes such a breadth of
meaning is born out by the specific teaching of many other
passages of Scripture. Amos, for example, accuses the mer-
chants of Israel of hardly being able to wait until they can
do business. They say to themselves, "When will the new
moon be over, that we may sell grain? And the sabbath,
that we may offer wheat for sale, that we may make the
ephah small and the shekel great, and deal deceitfully with
false balances . . . " (Amos 8:5). If we argue from Amos 8:5
alone that we should not steal anything we are engaging in
inductive reasoning (from the particular to the general). If
we argue from Exodus 20:15 alone that we should not
tamper with the scales, we are engaging in *deductive reasoning* (from the general to the particular). We saw illustrations of errors in the former way of reasoning in the previous chapter. Here we shall look at errors in the latter.

Misreading No. 13: Confused Definition
No deductive argument can proceed properly if we do not
have a clear concept of each term in the argument. For
example, if *stealing* in Exodus 20:15 does not mean something very general like "taking anything that is not right-
fully yours," then it cannot include tampering with scales.

An interesting case of just such an error is often made
when another of the Ten Commandments is involved.
Some readers, notably those with pacifist leanings, hold
that "Thou shalt not kill" (Ex. 20:13) forbids capital punishment. The term *kill,* so the argument goes, includes the
deadly force of police, army or court. But there are good
reasons for not interpreting this term so inclusively.

First among them is context.

Exodus 21:12-17 lists four crimes which require the death penalty; the first applies to premeditated murder: "Whoever strikes a man so that he dies shall be put to death. But if he did not lie in wait for him, but God let him fall into his hand, then I will appoint for you a place to which he may flee. But if a man willfully attacks another to kill him treacherously, you shall take him from my altar, that he may die" (Ex. 20:12-14). Later in the Old Testament the Israelites are commanded to take Canaan by deadly force. Either the Scriptures are contradictory—something non-Christians frequently charge—or "Thou shalt not kill" does not apply to capital punishment and at least some wars.

Old Testament scholar R. Alan Cole says, " 'Murder' is a good translation (RV, NEB)." And he then comments, "Certainly this command was never seen by Hebrews as ruling out the death penalty (Ex. 21:15). . . . Also, there were no pacifists in Old Testament days. Whether the fuller light of the New Testament demands such conclusions or not, they cannot be proved from the Old Testament alone."[1]

In the above argument we can see the intertwining of inductive and deductive reasoning. On the one hand, we cannot deduce pacifism from Exodus 20:13 or elsewhere in the Old Testament because by induction we can see Old Testament texts which do not fit. On the other hand, we might be able to argue for pacifism by induction, that is, by considering texts (in their context) from the New Testament. This is precisely the way many traditional Christians do in fact argue.

Case 1. Sometimes cult writers make basic errors in definition, errors so obvious that it is hard to believe they could have been made. Edgar Cayce, for example, once said during one of his "readings" that the Sadducees, a Jewish religious sect at the time of Jesus, did not believe in the resurrection. So far, so good. Then Cayce added for clarification, " 'There is no reincarnation'—which is what the word [*resurrection*] meant in those days."[2] But *resurrection* as the term is used in the New Testament has no relationship with the concept of reincarnation, as even a cursory look at the resurrection accounts in the Gospels and Acts and the comments of the apostle Paul in 1 Corinthians 15 will show. Reincarnation is the successive embodiment of the soul in a series of different mortal bodies; resurrection is the transformation of a person's one mortal body to an immortal one.

One of Cayce's followers also confused reincarnation with being "born again." Eula Allen is quoted as saying, "If you thought of reincarnation as rebirth, I think you could understand it better. Just as the earth has a constant rebirth [does she mean the annual cycle?] so does the spirit. Don't you remember Christ saying that 'Unless man is reborn again, he cannot enter the Kingdom of Heaven?' "[3] The verse quoted (though somewhat inaccurately; it's *born again* not *reborn again,* which is redundant) is John 3:3. Jesus' own explanation to Nicodemus who also was confused shows that reincarnation is not meant but rather a spiritual birth; each person who has been born physically must also be born spiritually in order to enter God's kingdom. There is no excuse for confusion, for the immediate context contains a definition which eliminates Eula Allen's interpretation.

Case 2. Another kind of *confused definition* results when ordinary biblical or theological terms are redefined within a system that is essentially foreign to the original context in which they appear. Arguments based on such definitions are hard to follow and move in a world quite divorced from the framework of the Bible.

For example, Mary Baker Eddy, as we have seen above, moves easily from plain biblical terms to eccentric, spiritual meanings on, as it appears, no particular basis but her own imagination. She explains the Trinity this way: "Life, Truth, and Love constitute the triune Person called God,— that is, the triply divine Principle, Love. They represent a trinity in unity, three in one,—the same in essence, though multiform in office: God the Father-Mother; Christ the spiritual idea of sonship; divine Science of the Holy Comforter. These three express in divine Science the three-fold, essential nature of the infinite. They also indicate the divine Principle of scientific being, the intelligent relation of God to man and the universe."[4] This passage is typical of *Science and Health with Key to the Scriptures.* Not only is no biblical reference given for this definition, no single, simple sense can be made of it. God is *Father-Mother;* Christ is the *spiritual idea of sonship;* the Holy Spirit is *divine Science.* But what do the words in italics mean?

In the paragraphs which follow, Mrs. Eddy does, in fact, take up the three—God, Christ and Holy Spirit—but one is still left confused as to their nature and character. Part of the reason for this is that to Eddy only Mind or Spirit is real; everything material or concrete in an earthly sense is unreal. But since the human mind understands matter far better than spirit, a sense of fuzziness and fog hangs over all her writing. Eddy explains this feeling, of course, by pointing out that our natural insistence that the material world is real is our basic error as human beings.

What is at issue is a fundamental presupposition about the nature of ultimate reality. Unlike Eddy, a traditional Christian claims that, though God is Spirit and he alone is self-existent (the really real), what he creates has reality too. The material world exists—really exists; it is his creation and it is good, at least in its original created state (Gen. 1). The doctrine of creation forever separates Christian Science from the biblical, Christian, world view.

Recognizing this fundamental difference between Christian Science and traditional Christianity is a start toward understanding Eddy's definitions of theological terms. It also explains why at least at first her terms seem so strange. But when we have noted the reason for these differences, we have not necessarily shown even to ourselves which system is true. This much we can say, however: reading Scripture on its own, without reference to Eddy's system is not likely to produce Eddy's interpretation. If we are to believe her own report, she was the first to discover this view anyway. Until 1866, no other Bible reader—Protestant, Catholic or agnostic—knew what Scripture really meant.[5]

Case 3. A third type of *confused definition* occurs when the testimony of Scripture is misunderstood or distorted to agree with a preconceived cultic view. Take, for example, the Jehovah's Witnesses' definition of the Holy Spirit. The Witnesses deny the traditional doctrine of the Trinity, not by turning the three persons into abstractions like the Christian Scientists' Life, Truth and Love, but by holding that Father, Son and Holy Spirit are not coequal. The Father alone is God. Jesus is "God's Son" and is not to be equated in deity with the Father.[6] And the Holy Spirit is not a person but a force: "The invisible active force of the Almighty God that moves his servants to do his will."[7]

The Scriptures were, for example, inspired by this force: "While men were used to write the Bible, they did so under the direction of God's powerful active force or holy spirit, so that 'all Scripture is inspired of God.' "[8] One notices here, too, that the word *holy spirit* is not capitalized as are Son of God and God the Father in Witness literature. This is true of the term as it appears throughout the New World Translation. A key verse for Trinitarians, for example, reads in the NWT: "Go therefore and make disciples of people of all nations, baptizing them in the name of the

Father and of the Son and of the holy spirit" (Mt. 28:19).

To explain this view of the Holy Spirit, the Witnesses argue that the words in the original Hebrew and Greek have been mistranslated "ghost" but should be translated "breath," "wind" or "breeze."[9] The Witnesses are in part correct, for these are clearly associated with the relevant Greek and Hebrew words.[10] But they fail to take into account the contexts in which those words appear in the Old and New Testaments.

Paul in Romans writes, for example, "When we cry, 'Abba! Father!' it is the Spirit himself bearing witness with our spirit that we are children of God" (8:15-16). Can a force (the holy spirit) bear witness with a force (a human spirit) in such a personal way that we cry, "Papa! Father!"? The NWT translates verse 16 this way: "The spirit itself bears witness with our spirit that we are God's children," thus depersonalizing the "spirit of God." But the context implies personality.

Another text relevant to the personhood of the Holy Spirit is Ephesians 4:30. "Do not grieve the Holy Spirit of God," Paul writes. How can one grieve a force? Resist it, yes; ignore it, yes; but grieve it, no.[11] The NWT, of course, translates the term in this verse in the lower case.

In the process of arriving at their definition of the Holy Spirit and translating the Bible, the Witnesses have ignored the full testimony of Scripture to the fact that the Holy Spirit is personal. In other words, along with confused definition (Misreading No. 13), they are guilty of selective citing (Misreading No. 11) and twisted translation (Misreading No. 2).

So we return to the point made earlier in this discussion: to understand Scripture we need to have a clear idea of its key terms. This is not always easy, especially where the terms apply to spiritual matters. Nonetheless, when such terms as *resurrection, born again* and *spirit* are taken in context and all the relevant Scriptures are brought to bear, a great deal becomes clear. We need not, therefore, as ordinary Christians defer to special spiritual experts, like Edgar Cayce or Mary Baker Eddy, to tell us what spiritual matters are really all about. We are responsible to check out all the experts' testimony for ourselves with the Scripture alone as our ultimate authority.

Misreading No. 14: Ignoring Alternative Explanations
Just as we can select evidence to justify our preconceived ideas we can ignore the alternative explanations for that evidence. We see a strange glowing light outside our window and if we have been susceptible to recent movies or television, we may suddenly conclude that we are seeing a flying saucer—maybe a space ship complete with extraterrestrial beings. But lots of things glow strangely in the dark—the full moon seen with your glasses off (well, at least, as seen by me with my glasses off), the headlight of a car seen through a forest, a campfire, a flashlight, the running lights of a commercial airliner and so on. To say you have just had a close encounter with the extraterrestrial without exhausting the other more ordinary explanations would be irresponsible if not irrational.

So, too, it is a fallacy to adopt an eccentric explanation when an ordinary one fits the data. At least, it is a fallacy to adopt it with a sense of certainty. Withholding judgment is required.

Case 1. Von Däniken opens his chapter, "Was God an Astronaut?" as follows: "The Bible is full of secrets and contradictions. Genesis, for example, begins with the creation of the earth, which is reported with absolute geological accuracy. But how did the chronicler know that minerals preceded plants and plants preceded animals?"[12]

A number of things strike the wary reader about this passage. First, the Bible has almost nothing to say about *geology.* Does von Däniken mean *biology* (it doesn't say much about that either)? Second, von Däniken declares the writer of Genesis a *chronicler.* But is Genesis 1 and 2 a chronicle or a poetic description of genuine cosmic events?

But our main interest here is in von Däniken's rhetorical question: "How did the chronicler know ... ?" Well, a Christian suggests, Genesis is revelation; it has been so understood by the ancient Hebrews, Jesus himself and the church down through the ages. The writer of Genesis, probably Moses, received his information from God: "In many and various ways God spoke of old to our fathers by the prophets" (Heb. 1:1). If divine revelation is taken as possible, then any degree of accuracy is at least in theory possible.

Von Däniken continues by quoting Genesis 1:26, " 'And God said, Let us make man in our image, after our likeness,' ... Why does God speak in the plural? Why does he say 'us,' not 'me,' why 'our,' and not 'my'? One would think that the one and only God ought to address mankind in the singular, not in the plural."[13] A quick look at almost any Bible commentary will produce at least two answers not involving God as a group of astronauts: (1) that "the Creator speaks as heaven's King accompanied by His heavenly hosts" or (2) that the plural prefigures the doctrine of the Trinity expressed more explicitly in the New Testament.[14] Both of these alternatives are consistent with the literary character of the text; von Däniken's implicit suggestion is not.

Case 2. The Mormon missionary manual contains another instance of ignoring alternative explanations. In order to convince "Mr. Brown," the prospective Mormon, that the Book of Mormon is the Word of God, the missionary is to say, "As you read each page of the Book of Mormon, pause and ponder. Ask yourself this question again and again: Could any man have written this book?"[15]

No other answer than the one intended is suggested. But, of course, several have been seriously proposed by those who have studied the life of Joseph Smith. Fawn Brodie, for example, concludes that Smith himself wrote it. George Arbaugh holds that its source is a novel originally drafted by Simon Spaulding and reworked prior to publication by Sidney Rigdon, Joseph Smith and Oliver Cawdrey. Hal Hougey suggests it derives from Ethan Smith's *View of the Hebrews*. And Harry Ropp wonders whether all of the theories may be in part true—that Smith used a number of sources.[16]

Once a controversy raged in literary circles in eighteenth-century England. A Scottish poet, James Macpherson, had claimed to find fragments of ancient epic poetry written by a bard called Ossian. Samuel Johnson, who long felt that this claim was fraudulent—Macpherson's attempt to get attention for his own poetic work—was once asked whether any man in the eighteenth century could have written such poems. He replied, "Yes, Sir, many men, many women, and many children."[17] The Mormon missionary manual never suggests that the prospective Mormon weigh any of the evidence for any alternate theories of the book's origin.

This particular fallacy may be easy to detect if the proposals are as strange as von Däniken's. But if they are only slightly awry—as in many readings given by the Jehovah's Witnesses (see, for example, their treatment of blood, pp. 84-88)—then more discernment is needed. The minimum requirement for that discernment is a basic knowledge of the general flow of Scripture and the pattern of its ideas. When an interpretation fails to fit into this flow and pattern, you should look more closely, consulting a commentary, perhaps. If you find other explanations for the text, you would do well to weigh all the evidence and all the explanations before adopting one as true or even more likely to be true than the others.

Misreading No. 15: The Obvious Fallacy
Interpretations of some biblical texts require great study.
Even then, honest scholars are uncertain and disagree with
each other. Yet we frequently find cult writers drawing
conclusions with great ease and expecting us to follow
their lead. The impression the interpreter wants to give
is that the case is closed. His view is the obvious one.

Case 1. Von Däniken again provides us with a striking
example.

Undoubtedly [my italics] the Ark [of the Covenant] was
electrically charged! If we reconstruct it today according
to the instructions handed down by Moses, an electrical
conductor of several hundred volts is produced. The
border and golden crown would have served to charge
the condenser which was formed by the gold plates and
a positive and negative conductor. If, in addition, one
of the two cherubim on the mercy seat acted as a magnet,
the loudspeaker—perhaps even a kind of set for communication between Moses and the spaceship—was
perfect. The details of the construction of the Ark of
the Covenant can be read in the Bible in their entirety.[18]
(Von Däniken does not give the reference, but Ex. 25:10-22
and 37:1-9 are probably what he has in mind.) The key
word here is *undoubtedly*. But we want to ask, Has von
Däniken built such an ark to check out his theory? How
did the cherubim get turned into a magnet? And how
would the loudspeaker that supposedly results work? I
know enough about electronics to be more than dubious.
The word *undoubtedly* here acts as a ploy to keep the reader
from thinking at all. Hurry over von Däniken's explanation and you are amazed at his theory; linger over it and
you are amazed at your own credulity.

Case 2. On a different topic entirely, we find the Jehovah's Witnesses also engaging in the obvious fallacy. "God's Word of truth tells us very clearly that we are fast nearing a worldwide change," says *The Truth That Leads to Eternal Life.*[19] As Christians we respond, "No, it doesn't. You can't move easily from scriptural prophecy to contemporary application. The Scripture does not *tell us very clearly* any such thing. If we are to draw such a conclusion, it will only be after much study of many texts whose particular application is not so clear.

Case 3. To repeat an illustration used earlier in connection with the meaning of the sticks in Ezekiel 37, the Mormon, James E. Talmage says, "*Plainly* the separate records of Judah and Joseph are here referred to."[20] But this connection is not *plain* at all. It makes at least as much sense to think of the sticks as representing the progeny of Judah and Joseph, as John B. Taylor does in his commentary.

Obviously, the way to avoid the obvious fallacy is to not be misled by the characterization any writer puts on the quality of his own argument. Look to see if it is so. Is the logic valid, the evidence all there? Is it treated fairly? Are alternatives acknowledged and refuted? One, then, should keep an eye out for subtle uses of these words and phrases that often mask poor or inadequate reasoning: *obviously, clearly, certainly, undoubtedly, no one can reasonably doubt, all reasonable people hold that, any intelligent person can see* and a host of variations.

A related fallacy occurs when one develops a series of interlinking, eccentric *possible* readings and then concludes that since these eccentric interpretations support each other, they must be *true*. Thus a series of speculations join together to achieve the strength of what appears to be an integrated world view. Actually, an interpretation which requires a number of possible meanings to be the actual ones is far less certain than any one of the possible readings taken alone.

Misreading No. 16: Virtue by Association

We have all heard of guilt by association. "Johnny must be a bad boy. Look at the company he keeps." Or, "How could Sarah be a Christian. Didn't I see her hanging out with that guy from Gary?"

This argument works in the other direction as well: "Billy goes to church. He's such a good boy." This is the way the argument is used by cult writers. If you can associate your view with Jesus, the Bible, the apostles, the patriarchs—any of the good guys of the Judeo-Christian tradition—you have enhanced the credibility of your argument. The fallacy itself takes several forms.

Case 1. One obvious form of *virtue by association* occurs when the cult writer associates Jesus with people on his list of worthies.

Mary Baker Eddy, for example, says that she won her way to "absolute conclusions through revelation, reason, and demonstration. . . . When a new spiritual idea is borne to earth, the prophetic Scripture of Isaiah is renewedly fulfilled: 'Unto us a child is born, . . . and his name shall be called Wonderful.' "[21] Thus she appropriates to herself and her system of religion the fulfillment of Isaiah's prophecy (Is. 9:6) and the glory of Jesus himself. Then she quotes Jesus' words implying that she, like him, teaches only what God the Father inspires: "My doctrine is not mine, but his that sent me" (Jn. 7:16 KJV).

Christmas Humphreys likens the Buddha to Jesus "who became Christos, the Christ, [who] was incarnate of the same Eternal Principle."[22] Rick Chapman in *How to Choose a Guru* lists twenty-one gurus that "you can't go wrong with." Along with Jesus are listed Christian figures (St. Francis and St. Theresa) and such others as Zoroaster, Krishna, Buddha, Meher Baba and Lao-tsu.[23] In a slightly different vein, the Mormon missionary manual recounts how Joseph Smith and Oliver Cowdrey went into the woods to pray and were visited by Peter, James and John who "gave them important power and authority from the Lord."[24] Thus in various ways the cult writers accredit their work or the cult's ideas.

Case 2. A second kind of virtue by association occurs when cult sources, or cult "scriptures" are likened to the Bible, the scriptures of other major religions or other highly reputable writings.

Juan Mascaro in his introduction to the Upanishads cites the New Testament, the Gospels, Ecclesiastes and Psalms, from which he quotes passages supposedly paralleling the Upanishads.[25] And the Maharishi Mahesh Yogi claims that not only Jesus taught that the kingdom of heaven is within you: "Bible teaches this, Vedas teach this, Upanishads teach, Gita teaches this, Islam teaches this, Buddhism teaches this, this fundamental experience."[26] Of course, the Maharishi takes the phrase ("The Kingdom of Heaven is within you") to mean Atman is Brahman or all is ultimately one. We have seen above that for Jesus and the Bible, this interpretation is incorrect. But how nice to imagine all those great scriptures and all those religions on your side!

Case 3. A far more subtle form of virtue by association occurs when cult literature imitates the form or directly quotes the words of Scripture but places these words in the context of ideas quite foreign to those involved in the original.

The Mormon scriptures are replete with examples. Turn almost at will to *Doctrine and Covenants* and one finds an illustration. Here is one: "Therefore, in the beginning the Word was, for he was the Word, even the messenger of salvation—the light and the Redeemer of the world; the Spirit of truth, who came into the world, because the world was made by him, and in him was the life of men and the light of men" *(Doctrine and Covenants 93:8-9).* This is a "re-

revelation" (my term) of John 1 with other phrases from elsewhere in the Gospel thrown in.

The passage above looks orthodox; after all it is a montage of phrases from John's Gospel. But note the following verses: "Man was also in the beginning with God. . . . For man is spirit. The elements are eternal, and spirit and element, inseparably connected, receive a fulness of joy" (93:33). We will examine below (pp. 141-43) the twist given to the original revelation by the rephrasing and totally new concepts that section 93 contains. The point here is the virtue these ideas receive by association with biblical phrasing and excerpts.

A similar feeling that cult revelation is authenticated comes when passages from the Bible are placed beside similar sounding passages from the Book of Mormon. The Mormon missionary manual, for example, speaks of Jesus' postresurrection appearances in the Gospels, referring to Matthew 28:1-10 and Luke 24:1-9. The missionary is to say, "Let's turn for a few moments to the Mormon account of the Savior's visit to the Americas."[27] Then 3 Nephi 11:7-10, 14 is quoted. This recounts an appearance of Christ to the Nephites. They first hear a voice: "Behold my Beloved Son, in whom I am well pleased, in whom I have glorified my name—hear ye him." Then they see a "Man descending out of heaven" who says to them, "Behold, I am Jesus Christ, whom the prophets testified shall come into the world. . . . Arise and come forth unto me, that ye may thrust your hands into my side, and also that ye may feel the prints of the nails in my hands and in my feet, that ye may know that I am the God of Israel, and the God of the whole earth, and have been slain for the sins of the world." The effect of putting biblical accounts alongside similar-sounding nonbiblical accounts is to lend credibility to the latter.

Sometimes style alone carries a sense of content. I well

remember a Sunday-evening sermon I once gave as a college student home for the summer. My text was Paul's letter to the Romans (the entire book!). To cover this and make it understandable I read copiously from Phillips' modern English version. One of the old saints of the church told me, frowning, "It just doesn't sound like the Bible." If I had read from the Book of Mormon, I might not have been given more than a puzzled expression in response.

Naming names, summoning up great witnesses, sounding like the Bible, proclaiming universality for your eccentric view—all these carry no logical weight unless what is said about them turns out on other grounds to be true. So we must be wary of any such attempt to authenticate eccentric religious doctrine.

Confused definition, ignoring alternative explanations, the obvious fallacy, virtue by association: this rather motley crew of misreadings all serve to befuddle people today. We do well not to also be misled by these errors in reasoning from Scripture.

Chapter 8
The Authority of the Bible

Among Protestant Christians the Bible—and the Bible alone *(sola Scriptura)*—is taken as the final authority in all matters of Christian life and thought. Summing up this tradition in a modern formulation, the Lausanne Covenant proclaims, "We affirm the divine inspiration, truthfulness and authority of both Old and New Testament Scriptures in their entirety as the only written word of God, without error in all that it affirms, and the only infallible rule of faith and practice" (Article 2).

Prior to the Reformation and Luther's and Calvin's insistence that the Bible alone is our authority, the Roman Catholic Church had developed a twofold approach to religious authority. The Bible was basic, but what the Bible meant was determined by the church in accordance with tradition. In other words, the current ecclesiastical hierarchy (one's priest, bishop, archbishop and finally the pope himself, especially in his official capacity as head of the church) mediated the interpretation of the Bible by reference to the body of commentary and teaching that was growing over the centuries, the teaching of the early church Fathers and so on. Luther came hard up against this approach to authority when he tried, as a university professor and priest, to convince the church that salvation came by grace alone *(sola gratia)* through faith alone *(sola fides)*. It was out of this struggle that the question of authority came to the fore.

Luther's words at the Diet of Worms are a famous encapsuling of the principle which was to become so important to the success of the Protestant cause: "Unless I am convicted by Scripture and plain reason—I do not accept the authority of popes and councils, for they have contradicted each other—my conscience is captive to the Word of God, I cannot and I will not recant anything, for to go against conscience is neither right nor safe. God help me. Amen."[1] Three touchstones are involved here. First is Scripture alone as authority.

Second is "plain reason" as one's guide to what Scripture means. Luther does not hold human reason over Scripture as a judge of what it *can* say but as a tool to discover what it *does* say; and what it does say is true whether it otherwise fits human reason or not. Thus the coequality of God the Father, God the Son and God the Holy Spirit—while, perhaps not totally understood by human reason—is nonetheless the teaching of Scripture as best we can determine, following the ordinary meaning of the language of Scripture.

The third touchstone is Luther's conscience. As an individual person Luther must not go against what he himself sincerely understands Scripture to mean.

Luther was not anxious to throw out centuries of Christian thought and scholarship simply because it was not his own. But he insisted that if the church Fathers or popes wanted the church to hold a certain doctrine or engage in a certain practice they must rely solely on Scripture for their authority.

This bit of church history is relevant to our concerns in this chapter: the development of esoteric interpretation, the esoteric addenda or alternatives to the Bible and the occult and cultic challenges to the authority of Scripture.

Misreading No. 17: Esoteric Interpretation

I begin with the *esoteric interpretation* because it presents itself as a way of understanding the true, spiritual meaning of the Scriptures.[2] As Mary Baker Eddy says, "The one important interpretation of Scripture is the spiritual."[3]

The esoteric tradition boasts a long history.[4] Its exponents frequently trace it back to the Essenes (a Jewish sect that preserved the Dead Sea Scrolls), the Gnostics of the New Testament era and even to Jesus himself who said, "I have yet many things to say to you, but you cannot hear them now. When the Spirit of truth comes, he will guide you into all the truth" (Jn. 16:12-13).[5] Whether the current exponents of the tradition are teaching anything like the Essenes and other early forebears is, however, questionable.[6] Of course, our task is not to examine issues of history but to understand the tradition so that we can detect and avoid errors associated with it.

Two separate but related strains in the esoteric tradition concern us. The first is the notion that the Bible—and many other religious and nonreligious texts—contains a secret, hidden, inner meaning that can only be spiritually discerned, what I call *the esoteric interpretation* (Misreading No. 17). The second is the practice not only of divining the hidden meaning of already existing texts but of receiving new revelation, special communication from the Other

Side which tells us new information about reality and even about Jesus—*supplementing biblical authority* (Misreading No. 18).

Esoteric interpretation assumes that the Bible does not mean what it says on the surface. As Madam Helena Petrovna Blavatsky, the late nineteenth-century founder of the Theosophical Society, says in *Isis Unveiled,* "The greatest teachers of divinity agree that nearly all ancient books were written symbolically and in a language intelligible only to the initiated."[7] Unless one has the special insight given only to the few, the elite, one will remain forever on the outside. Manly Palmer Hall says, "Today there are innumerable truths which remain unrevealed to the seeker after knowledge because he does not possess the philosophic *open-sesame.*"[8]

But how does one become one of the elite capable of discerning the hidden meaning of these ancient texts? Marc Edmund Jones in *Occult Philosophy,* a helpful introduction to the occult world view, gives some perspective. He describes how an occultist "seeks to establish himself as a spiritual figure of importance to the race":

Whether the conscious charlatan, or merely megalomaniac to greater or lesser degree, he first claims instruction or approval by the elders—directly or through clairvoyant means—and then seeks by actual or imaginary great travels about the globe to collect the pearls of wisdom which he offers to the faithful. The pattern is not rendered invalid by any such counterfeit of its characteristics, however, and there is a *bona fide* relation of teacher and pupil to be found in all spiritual reality, together with every sort of broadening experience in meeting the diversity of human minds. . . .

The investigator without background in the field is often baffled very understandably at this point. He must realize that the average esotericist is little inclined to make a distinction between a purely subjective and an actually objective experience. What to the outsider would be nothing more than imagination will constitute an effective astral functioning for a disciple of ancient mysteries, especially when it comes to instruction from the elders and the journey for supposedly eternal knowledge.[9]

Jones's comments are instructive: the confirmation of spiritual discernment may well be only subjective. No attempt is made to use "actually objective experience" as a measure for inner spiritual reality.

Put in Luther's terms, this makes the *conscience* not only the seat of conviction but the whole of *consciousness*, in fact, the generator of the content of consciousness. Luther, however, relied on Scripture alone as the source of the content of consciousness. The Bible was an objective, *outside* source, common to all readers—Luther and his fellow Christians. And Scripture was to be understood through a person's intellectual capacity, an aspect of the image of God each person bears. Luther could trust his own ability because God himself stood behind that ability as its Creator.

We will turn now to examples of *esoteric interpretation* within the Christian tradition.

Case 1. Emanuel Swedenborg (1688-1772) may be a name unfamiliar to most people today. While the religious organization which developed around his teaching, The Church of the New Jerusalem, is still in existence, in the United States it is small and its influence minor.[10] In his own day, however, Swedenborg was a dynamic figure, an important Swedish intellectual and religious force. The poet William Blake was influenced by him. And even the philosopher Immanuel Kant, who was fascinated by his psychic abilities, devoted a small treatise to him.[11]

What makes Swedenborg interesting to us is that he represents an almost pure strain of esotericism within a gen-

erally Christian frame of reference. Swedenborg's father
was a Lutheran bishop, and the brilliant young Swedenborg grew up with a sense of religious and intellectual
curiosity. While Swedenborg was intent in his early studies
to "discover the soul," he took the tack of mechanistic science as it was developing in the early eighteenth century.[12]
Swedenborg wrote a number of learned scientific, philosophic and religious treatises, taking a traditional stance
toward the Christian faith. But something dramatic happened in 1743, when Swedenborg was fifty-two years old.
Whereas, for example, he had understood the Genesis creation account as literal history, he now regarded it as "a
Divine allegory, the only consistent interpretation of which
is shown to be spiritual."[13]

Swedenborg himself explained what happened: ". . . It is
expedient here to premise, that, of the Lord's Divine
mercy, it has been granted me, now for several years, to be
constantly and uninterruptedly in company with spirits and
angels, hearing them converse with each other, and con-
versing with them. Hence it has been permitted me to hear
and see things in another life which are astonishing, and
which have never before come to the knowledge of any
man, nor entered into his imagination."[14] Swedenborg
then goes on to list the topics on which he has received
special insight: the various kinds of spirits, the state of souls
after death and the "doctrine of faith which is acknowledged throughout all heaven." As this book and Swedenborg's immense output of future publications reveal, the
doctrines he now espouses are far from orthodox.[15]

Swedenborg's treatment of the Bible, as an example of
esoteric interpretation, is seen in his hermeneutic: "In its
first origin the Word is purely Divine; when this passed
through the Heavens of the Lord's Celestial Kingdom it
was Divine Celestial, and when it passed through the Heavens of the Lord's Spiritual Kingdom it was Divine Spiritual,

and when it came to man it became Divine Natural; hence it is that the natural sense of the Word contains within it the spiritual sense, and thus the celestial sense, and both a purely Divine, which is not open to any man, nor even to an angel."[16] To Swedenborg, then, there are four levels of meaning: (1) natural, (2) spiritual, (3) celestial and (4) purely divine. No man nor angel can penetrate to the final level.[17]

How does this hermeneutic work out in practice? Of course, the purely divine is not open to him, and from what I have read in his works, it would seem that Swedenborg leaves the celestial level to the angels. But he does expend great effort giving the spiritual meaning of Scripture. Here is an example of his exegesis of Matthew 24:29-31. We will quote the passage as it appears in the English translation of *Heaven and Its Wonders and Hell:*

> "Immediately after the tribulation of those days the sun shall be darkened, and the moon shall not give her light, and the stars shall fall from heaven, and the powers of the heavens shall be shaken. And then shall appear the sign of the Son of man in heaven; and then shall all the tribes of the earth mourn; and they shall see the Son of man coming in the clouds of heaven with power and great glory. And He shall send forth His angels with a trumpet and a great sound; and they shall gather together His elect from the four winds, from the end of the heavens even to the end thereof" (Matt. xxiv. 29-31).

Those who understand these words according to the sense of the letter have no other belief than that during that closing period, which is called the final judgment, all these things are to occur as they are described in the literal sense. . . . Such is the belief of most men in the church at the present day.

But those who so believe are ignorant of the arcana

that lie hid in every particular of the Word. For in every
particular of the Word there is an internal sense which
treats of things spiritual and heavenly, not of things
natural and worldly which are treated of in the sense of
the letter. And this is true not only of the general meaning of many expressions, it is true of every single expression. . . .

It is according to that sense that what the Lord says in
the words quoted above respecting His coming in the
clouds of heaven must be understood. The "sun" there
that is to be darkened signifies the Lord in respect to
love; the "moon" the Lord in respect to faith; "stars"
knowledges of good and truth, or of love and faith; "the
sign of the Son of man in heaven" the manifestation of
Divine truth; "the tribes of the earth" that shall mourn,
all things relating to truth and good or to faith and love;
"the coming of the Lord in the clouds of heaven with
power and glory" His presence in the Word, and revelation, "clouds" signifying the sense of the letter of the
Word, and "glory" the internal sense of the Word; "the
angels with a trumpet and a great sound" signify heaven
as a source of Divine truth. From the meaning of these
words of the Lord it is evident that at the end of the
church, when there is no longer any love, and consequently no faith, the Lord will open the internal meaning
of the Word and reveal arcana of heaven. . . .[18]

Swedenborg goes on to justify this spiritual reading of
Matthew by pointing out that people in his day know very
little about heaven, hell and the afterlife. They do not know
that anyone has ever come from that world to tell us. He
comments,

Lest, therefore, such a spirit of denial, which especially
prevails with those who have much worldly wisdom,
should also infect and corrupt the simple in heart and the
simple in faith, it has been granted to me to associate

with angels and to talk with them as man with man, also
to see what is in the heavens and what is in the hells, and
this for thirteen years; also from what I have thus heard
and seen I am now permitted to describe these, in the
hope that ignorance may thus be enlightened and unbe-
lief dissipated. Such immediate revelation is granted at
this day because this is what is meant by the Coming of
the Lord.[19]

Though, according to George Trobridge, Swedenborg
claimed that the natural or literal sense of Scripture was
and should be the basis of the church's doctrine, nonetheless this literal sense is "often obscure and misleading."
Thus one does not read far into a book by Swedenborg written after 1749 which does not soon diverge from orthodoxy.

Swedenborg is not so much engaging in exegesis according to an interpretive principle as seeing Scripture solely
in the light of his conversations with the angels. Those of
us without his insight can have nothing to say about such
readings; we can only wonder at them and accept them or
reject them. They have only as much authority as Swedenborg himself.

What an irony it is that in 1937 a schism occurred in The
Church of the New Jerusalem! Some members held that
since the writings of Swedenborg were "the Word of the
Lord" they must have an internal sense, too, one which only
an elite would understand! Others disagreed. Thus the
rift.[20] This, then, is the key to the fallacy of esoteric interpretation. It is totally private. There is no way to check it
out. There is no way to tell if the system that derives from
esotericism is really so or merely a figment of the esotericist's imagination—or worse—a direct plant by the
Father of Lies.[21]

To the traditional Christian, of course, only one response is possible—rejection of the system. The apostle
Paul was quite clear: "Even if we, or an angel from heaven,

should preach to you another gospel contrary to that which we preached to you, let him be accursed" (Gal. 1:8).

Case 2. Christian Science also fits into the esoteric tradition for Mary Baker Eddy, too, emphasizes the spiritual meaning of Scripture. Her ability to discern this meaning and the system deriving from it, she says, were given to her by God: "In the year 1866, I discovered the Christ Science or divine laws of Life, Truth, and Love, and named my discovery Christian Science. God had been graciously preparing me during many years for the reception of this final revelation of the absolute divine Principle of scientific mental healing. . . . I won my way to absolute conclusions through divine revelation, reason and demonstration."[22] And she adds, "In following these leadings, the Bible was my only textbook. The Scriptures were illumined; reason and revelation were reconciled, and afterwards the truth of Christian Science was demonstrated."[23]

We have already seen how Eddy gave spiritual definitions to ordinary words like *morning, evening* and *day* (see pp. 66-68), thereby triggering a spiritual interpretation of Genesis, for example. Here is her spiritual interpretation of the Lord's Prayer (Mt. 6:9-13):

Our Father which art in heaven,
Our Father-Mother God, all-harmonious,
Hallowed be Thy name.
Adorable One.
Thy kingdom come.
Thy kingdom is come; Thou art ever-present.
Thy will be done in earth, as it is in heaven.
Enable us to know,—as in heaven, so on earth,—
God is omnipotent, supreme.
Give us this day our daily bread;
Give us grace for to-day; feed the famished affections;
And forgive us our debts, as we forgive our debtors.
And Love is reflected in love;

And lead us not into temptation, but deliver us from evil;
*And God leadeth us not into temptation, but delivereth
us from sin, disease, and death.*
For Thine is the kingdom, and the power, and the
glory, forever.
*For God is infinite, all-power, all Life, Truth, Love, over
all, and All.*
As with Swedenborg there is no way one can logically derive this meaning from the passage. That is, no principle of reading is involved. One either accepts the spiritual sense as given by Eddy or rejects it. One might, of course, wonder whether Eddy's spiritual reading of Genesis squares with Swedenborg's spiritual reading. A quick check shows that they are as unlike each other as each is from the passage they are both interpreting.[24]

We can note, therefore, what happens when the perspicuity of the Scriptures is allowed to atrophy. As we saw in chapter one, the Bible can be understood by ordinary people with ordinary intelligence. We do not need a Swedenborg or a Mary Baker Eddy to give us special insight hidden to the rest of us. In fact, when such "insight" disagrees with the plain sense of Scripture, the Scripture has already specifically told us to reject it.

Misreading No. 18: Supplementing Biblical Authority
The second strain in the esoteric tradition is not just to discern new spiritual meanings to old scriptural texts but to supplement the Bible with new revelation or to add authorities other than revelation as such.

Case 1. Archie Matson, for example, combines two further authorities with the Bible, both of which he considers more certain in their information. Science, the first of these authorities, has "largely won [the battle with the Bible] in the fields of physical and biological science."[25] Mediumship, the second of these authorities, is "the crown which gives confirmation and clarity to all the rest [various evidence from deathbed scenes, apparitions, the Bible and science]. None of them, not even the Bible, could carry conviction to the modern mind standing by itself."[26] Thus throughout his book *Afterlife,* the testimony of Scripture is weighed against that of science and mediumship.

Case 2. Using the extrabiblical authority of his own power as a medium, Edgar Cayce supplemented the Bible's account of creation, the Incarnation, life of Jesus and the history of the church. In addition, of course, he added stories of Egypt, Persia and the lost civilization of Atlantis.

Much of this material directly contradicts the Bible. Cayce, for example, once was asked, "When did the knowledge come to Jesus that He was to be the Savior of the world?" And he answered, "When he fell in Eden."[27] Jesus, he taught, possibly had "some thirty incarnations during His development in becoming The Christ."[28] The Virgin Mary "was the twin soul of the Master in the entrance into the earth! . . . Neither Mary nor Jesus had a human father. They were *one* soul so far as earth is concerned."[29]

Case 3. The Mormons, of course, are an important example of those who supplement the Bible with other authorities. Not only do they add the Book of Mormon, the *Doctrine and Covenants* and the *Pearl of Great Price,* they also have a "living prophet," the head of the Mormon church through whom revelation still comes.[30]

The Bible actually seems to have little practical value in the day-to-day teaching of the Mormon church. The reason for this is not hard to find. First, the clear documentation to their distinctive doctrines is all drawn from their other scriptures.[31]

Second, they believe that the Bible contains errors not found in the other scriptures. Joseph Fielding Smith says, for example: "We are all aware that there are errors in the *Bible* due to faulty translations and ignorance on the part of translators; but *the hand of the Lord has been over this volume of scripture* nevertheless, and *it is remarkable that it has come down to us in the excellent condition in which we find it.* Guided by the *Book of Mormon, Doctrine and Covenants* and the Spirit of the Lord, it is not difficult for one to discern the errors in the *Bible*" (italics his).[32] So the Bible's authority is actually played down, for wherever it teaches something differing from *Doctrine and Covenants,* for example, *Doctrine and Covenants* is accepted as true and the Bible as mistranslated.

Case 4. To Sun Myung Moon and the Unification Church the Bible, or at least parts of it, is "an actual revelation from God," but it is not complete nor fully accurate.[33] "The Bible is not the truth itself but a textbook teaching us the truth."[34] It is open to so many different interpretations that confusion such as that shown in the diversity of denominations is bound to result. What is needed is "a new truth that can elucidate the fundamental contents of the Bible so clearly that everyone can recognize and agree with it."[35] The implication here is that *Divine Principle* is that new truth.

This is confirmed by the "General Introduction" to the book: "This new truth has already appeared. With the fullness of time, God sent His messenger to resolve the fundamental questions of life and the universe. His name is Sun Myung Moon. For many decades, he wandered in a vast spiritual world in search of the ultimate truth.... He came in contact with many saints in Paradise and with Jesus, and thus brought into light all the heavenly secrets through his communication with God."[36] In fact, the introduction says that *Divine Principle* is only "part of the new truth" and that the hope is that more and deeper insights will follow and that "the light of truth will quickly fill the earth."[37] Part of the Unification Church's use of the Bible is clearly rhetorical. As Moon himself says, "Until our mission with the Christian church is over, we must quote the Bible and use it to explain the *Divine Principle*. After we receive the inheritance of the Christian church, we will be free to teach without the bible."[38]

Divine Principle suggests that at least some of Moon's disciples will themselves be able to see and commune with spirit-men (those who have died but not yet reached spiritual maturity) and even such departed saints as John the Baptist.[39] In this way *Divine Principle* itself both supplements the Bible and encourages its readers to supplement it further on their own.

With supplementing biblical authority we have reached the logical end of all misreadings. As we will soon see, Jesus put the Old Testament in the highest position of authority. The New Testament follows in that vein.[40] Now we see the results of putting that authority aside. The visions of the mediums go beyond the teaching of the Bible, contradicting both the Bible and each other. The teachings of the new prophets—Joseph Smith, Edgar Cayce, Mary Baker Eddy, Sun Myung Moon—are a strange mixture of the obvious, the bizarre, the grotesque and the incredible. The Bible never feels so powerful and so true than after one has been reading the accounts of this world's visionaries.

Misreading No. 19: Rejecting Biblical Authority
Rejecting biblical authority is not so much a mistake in reading as an attitude one takes before beginning to read or, perhaps, a conclusion one comes to after reading. One does not have to look far today for challenges to the authority of Scripture. Our secular age is dominated by naturalist assumptions. Either there is no God and hence no revelation, or God is an impersonal force or First Cause or Ultimate Energy which got things going in the cosmos but is not concerned personally with the result.

Case 1. An early exponent of this attitude in biblical study was Ernest Renan who in his introduction to *The Life of Jesus* wrote, "Until a new order of things prevails, we shall maintain then this principle of historical criticism—that a supernatural account cannot be admitted as such, that it always implies credulity or imposture, that the duty of the historian is to explain it, and seek to ascertain what share of truth or of error it may conceal."[41] He then began the "life" itself with this sentence: "Jesus was born at Nazareth, a small town of Galilee, which before his time had no celebrity," thus rejecting as legend the Bethlehem narratives and causing a furor among his readers.[42] Renan's skepticism regarding miracles has remained a feature of the modern world. It is reflected, for example, in such "naturalistic cult" literature as von Däniken's *Chariot of the Gods.* (See pp. 78-79, 83-84 and 96-97.) He represents well the naturalistic presuppositions in some twentieth-century cult literature. If God exists, of course, the naturalist's case is lost.

But there are serious challenges to biblical authority that are not necessarily based on naturalist presuppositions. Some focus on alleged contradictions in the Bible, a charge that over the last few centuries has been especially prevalent. The accusation takes many forms, each of which needs to be dealt with separately, something we cannot take space here to do. We will look in detail at only one example.

Case 2. Archie Matson holds that the Bible does "contain the word of God," but he attacks the ultimate authority of the Bible on three fronts. First, he claims that the Bible as taken literally is "so obviously false that we need not belabor the matter."[43] Thus he commits the obvious fallacy and caricatures the position maintained by traditional Christians and the author of the present book. He gives as reasons the inapplicability of the sanitary regulations of Leviticus and Paul's preaching about women wearing hats

in church. These are not, of course, serious objections to
the traditional view of Scripture, for that view takes into
account the relevance of literary, historical and cultural
context to the contemporary application of Scripture.

Second, he uses innuendo to impugn the integrity of
Scripture: "Commands to massacre and blessings on
murder are both there along with orders to eat no pork
and to stone blasphemers. What a book!"[44] Again there
is a total disregard for literary and historical context in his
implied charge.

Third, he claims that the Bible contradicts itself in many
areas. We will look in detail at one important example of
such alleged contradictions. Matson uses Jesus himself as
his authority for rejecting Scripture as the final authority.
"Actually we can take the Bible as the word of God only
by thinking of it as a book of religion, and interpreting
each part of it in the light of the life and character of the
Master. While he knew and loved the Old Testament, he
did not hesitate to quote it six times in one chapter of his
most famous sermon; and then to contradict it each time
with his 'but I say unto you'. (Matthew 5)"[45] Matson makes
no further comment on this. He just goes on to other matters, leaving the sting of this challenge to work its effect.

An examination of the Bible, however, shows that
Matson has misrepresented Jesus' teaching in the Sermon
on the Mount. I will take longer in dealing with this issue
than I have with most others in this book. The reason is
that the matter could not be more crucial. If Jesus dis-
trusted the Old Testament, contradicting the prophets
whom it claims as God's messengers, then we as Christians
do not have the solid basis for our beliefs that we have
always thought. So let us turn, then, to Jesus' comments
on Scripture in the Sermon on the Mount.

First, Jesus prefaces his "but I say unto you" phrases
with the following general comment about the Old Testa-

ment: "Think not that I have come to abolish the law and the prophets; I have come not to abolish them but to fulfil them. For truly, I say to you, till heaven and earth pass away, not an iota, not a dot, will pass from the law until all is accomplished" (Mt. 5:17-18). Jesus did more than just "know and love" (Matson's phrase) the Old Testament. Many people "know and love" Shakespeare's plays, but they don't consider them so authoritative that "not an iota, not a dot" will pass away until they are "accomplished."

Second, Matson misrepresents the meaning of "but I say unto you." Matson implies that Jesus uses it to mean that he is opposed to the Old Testament. But when we look at what Jesus actually says, we find something quite different. Note especially the following:

> You have heard that it was said to the men of old, "You shall not kill; and whoever kills shall be liable to judgment" [Ex. 20:13]. *But I say to you* that every one who is angry with his brother shall be liable to judgment; whoever insults his brother shall be liable to the council, and whoever says, "You fool!" shall be liable to the hell of fire. (Mt. 5:21-22)

> You have heard that it was said, "You shall not commit adultery" [Ex. 20:14]. *But I say to you* that everyone who looks at a woman lustfully has already committed adultery with her in his heart. (Mt. 5:27-28)

> It was also said, "whoever divorces his wife, let him give her a certificate of divorce" [Deut. 24:1-4]. *But I say to you* that every one who divorces his wife, except on the ground of unchastity, makes her an adulteress; and whoever marries a divorced woman commits adultery. (Mt. 5:31-32)

Here Jesus' phrase "but I say to you" is not used to *contradict* but to *expand* and *qualify*. Jesus is giving further teaching, in the first two instances, showing that there is an inner nature to sin. It is not just external acts that matter, but one's thoughts and motives. In the third instance, Jesus was limiting the scope of acceptable cases of divorce, not contradicting the earlier law.

The following three uses of the phrase "but I say to you" need special attention. At first Matson may seem to have a case.

> Again you have heard that it was said to the men of old, "You shall not swear falsely, but shall perform to the Lord what you have sworn" [Lev. 19:12; Num. 30:2; Deut. 23:21-23]. *But I say to you,* Do not swear at all, either by heaven, for it is the throne of God, or by the earth, for it is his footstool, or by Jerusalem, for it is the city of the great King. And do not swear by your head, for you cannot make one hair white or black. Let what you say be simply "Yes" or "No"; anything more than this comes from evil. (Mt. 5:33-37)

While it would appear that Jesus is contradicting the Old Testament, when we examine the passages he quotes we find that their emphasis is identical to that of Jesus. The Old Testament does not command one to swear. Rather it states that, if one swears, one *must* perform what he has sworn to perform. Then, of course, he adds that swearing by some holy thing or other should itself be avoided. A Christian is simply to be honest and straightforward on the basis of his own character and settled conviction to obey God. It is not necessary to "swear" by anything.

If we see Jesus' comments on swearing in the larger context of Matthew's Gospel we get a further glimpse of why Jesus was so opposed to swearing. From Matthew 23:16-22 we see that the Pharisees had been using loopholes to avoid doing what they had promised. Jesus charges, "Woe to you, blind guides, who say, 'If any one swears by the temple, it is nothing; but if any one swears by the gold of the temple, he is bound by his oath.' You blind fools! For which is greater, the gold or the temple that has made the gold sacred?" (Mt. 23:16-17). And he goes on to give in verses 18-19 a further example of their sophistry, concluding that all oaths are to be taken with ultimate seriousness. There is no way one can sneak out of a commitment without violating the law of God. We conclude, then, that here too Matson is incorrect to think that Jesus has contradicted the Old Testament.

So we turn to the fifth passage in question.

You have heard that it was said, "An eye for an eye and a tooth for a tooth" [Ex. 21:24; Lev. 24:20; Deut. 19:21]. *But I say to you,* Do not resist one who is evil. But if anyone strikes you on the right cheek, turn to him the other also; and if any one would sue you and take your coat, let him have your cloak as well; and if any one forces you to go one mile, go with him two miles. (Mt. 5:38-41)

Again upon analysis we find that no contradiction is intended. The Old Testament passages are directed to the theocratic society of Israel. The point of such laws as an "eye for an eye" was twofold. First, it affirmed the value of the eye of the victim. One cannot arbitrarily destroy the property of another or mutilate his person. People are important. Second, this sort of law gave a measure of justice. If one eye was destroyed, justice does not demand two eyes from the offender. As a restraint on revenge it blends well with Jesus' further restraints.

In the Sermon on the Mount, however, Jesus directs his remarks not to society but to the offended person or persons. If someone offends you, you are not supposed to fight back. You cannot excuse a violent response on the basis of revenge or retaliation. Jesus' disciples are not to insist on justice for themselves but to exercise love and mercy.

This very point is at the heart of the sixth passage in

question. Jesus goes on to say,

> You have heard that it was said, "You shall love your
> neighbor and hate your enemy." *But I say to you,* Love
> your enemies and pray for those who persecute you, so
> that you may be sons of your Father who is in heaven;
> for he makes his sun rise on the evil and on the good,
> and sends rain on the just and on the unjust.... You,
> therefore, must be perfect, as your heavenly Father is
> perfect. (Mt. 5:43-45, 48)

Here Matson would seem to have a point. Jesus' "but I say
to you" is used in the sense of contradiction. But what does
Jesus contradict? He does not contradict the phrase "you
shall love your neighbor" which is a direct quote from
Leviticus 19:18. What he contradicts is the so-called command "to hate your enemies." Yet we search in vain in
the Old Testament for such a command.[45] Jesus was contradicting a perversion of God's law, probably a popular
one. What Jesus' listeners had "heard said" in this case was
not from the Scriptures at all.

So where does this leave Matson's challenge to biblical
authority? On no grounds at all, at least with regard to
this charge that the Master himself couldn't accept the
Scriptures. Not only could he accept them; he showed his
contemporaries—and anyone else who has listened since
then to his words in Scripture—just how important those
Scriptures were. They were to be treated with respect—
learned and obeyed—not only according to the letter but
according to their spirit.

Captive to the Word of God

Where did you get that idea? What is your authority?
What evidence do you have for relying on this authority?
These are crucial questions and we should be thankful to
the person who challenges us with them. For if we haven't
thought through why we believe, what we believe can

easily fall prey to any attractive idea that comes along.

Esoteric interpretation can lead us far away from the biblical pattern of thought. Supplementing that authority with other religious texts or with the teachings and visions of current gurus can lead us even further until we may, like Matson, challenge biblical authority or, like many modern cults such as the International Society for Krishna Consciousness (the Hare Krishnas) reject biblical authority completely.

Let us affirm again with Luther, that unless "we are convinced by Scripture and plain reason" we will not be led into any new religious beliefs. Rather let our consciences be "captive to the Word of God."

Chapter 9

World-View Confusion: The Heart of the Matter

We come finally to the most fundamental misreading of all. Or rather we return to it, having already introduced the concept in chapter two. World-view confusion is either the major cause or the major result of all other reading errors. For what is at stake is the overall pattern of meaning that distinguishes one cult from another, one religion from another, one world view from another.

When the Maharishi Mahesh Yogi attributes the psalmist's "Be still, and know that I am God" to Jesus and then proceeds to give the sentence a meaning that fits Hinduism but contrasts with Judaism and Christianity, he is co-opting Jesus and the psalmist for himself. To the unwary he makes a strong case, for the unwary do not know that Jesus did not say those words and that those words were intended to mean something diametrically opposed to the Maharishi's teaching. World-view confusion here works very well for the cult leader.

But the issue involved in the words "Be still, and know that I am God" is so fundamental that salvation itself depends on how we understand them. If we hold with the Maharishi that we are Godhood, we are rejecting the truth that we are God's creation, fallen, sinful and in desperate need of God's grace in Jesus Christ. We cannot have both God's forgiveness from our sin of pride and a self-concept of our own Godhood. The Maharishi's teaching is, in the words of the apostle Paul, "a different gospel" (Gal. 1:6). If world-view confusion can be this misleading, we need to take a much closer look at how it functions in Bible reading.

Misreading No. 20: World-View Confusion
World-view confusion, as we saw in chapter two, occurs whenever a reader of Scripture fails to interpret the Bible within the intellectual and broadly cultural framework of the Bible itself but uses instead a foreign frame of reference. The usual way in which it appears is for scriptural statements, stories, commands or symbols which have a particular meaning or set of related meanings within the biblical frame of reference to be lifted out and placed within another frame of reference. The result is that the original, intended meaning is lost or distorted, and a new and quite different meaning is substituted.

I have dealt with three examples of world-view confusion involving Eastern thought in chapter two (pp. 28-30) and noted as well the world-view confusion in the Mormon teaching concerning the premortal existence of human beings (pp. 59-61).

In all the cases noted so far an important principle of responsible reading has been violated: We should always read in the spirit of the writer, pay attention to what the writer has actually said in the cultural and intellectual framework natural to the text. That is, a good reader always sees the text in terms of its original historical and literary context.

Not to do this when reading the Bible is not only to violate the literary character of Scripture but to confuse the very systems of thought that underlie human discourse. To read a text out of context is to violate the integrity of the original writer and to set up one's own frame of reference as the arbitrary absolute into which any sentence by anybody must fit. Who cares what the psalmist meant when he said, "Be still, and know that I am God"? If the sentence can be made to function in my own frame of reference with my own meaning, then I will use it as I choose.

As harsh as this analysis sounds, I think it describes exactly the attitude and practice of many cult writers (and, for that matter, often many Christians as well in addressing some issues). They assume that such and such an idea is true. Then they look at the Bible to see if they can find something that sounds like it confirms this idea. I do not know how else to explain the Mormon reading of the stick of Judah as the Bible and the stick of Joseph as the Book of Mormon in Ezekiel 37 (see pp. 71-74). There are far more contextually natural ways of understanding the prophecy.

Or take Alan Watts's statement that Jesus was accusing the religious leaders of overvaluing the Scripture when he said, "You search the scriptures, because you *think* that in them you have eternal life" (Jn. 5:39). The completion of this very sentence shows that Jesus was upholding those Scriptures: "and it is they that bear witness to me; yet you refuse to come to me that you may have life" (vv. 39-40). But Watts did not quote that. Watts was not trying to explain what the Gospel of John was saying. He was lifting out part of a conversation and making it mean something directly opposite by putting it in his own context (see pp. 56-58).

In the remainder of this chapter we will examine in some depth several important examples of world-view confusion. First we will look at a cult theology in which world-view confusion lies at the very heart of its approach to Scripture.

Second, we will focus on the radically different ways in which the opening verses of the Gospel of John have been understood by traditional Christians, by Sun Myung Moon, by the Jehovah's Witnesses and by the Mormons. This analysis will show how when one changes the master system into which a biblical text fits, one changes the meaning that the text itself seems to convey.

Cult Theology and World-View Confusion
One of the clearest examples of world-view confusion at work throughout a whole theological treatise is found in *Divine Principle,* the primary expression of the thought of Sun Myung Moon. For Unificationists, *Divine Principle* is "the present truth and supercedes Christian theology."[1] As the "General Introduction" to *Divine Principle* puts it, "Scripture can be likened to a lamp which illuminates the truth. Its mission is to shed the light of truth. When a brighter light appears, the mission of the old one fades."[2] So the new teachings of Moon replace the Bible.

Divine Principle, originally written in Korean, presents a system of theology which begins with the nature and character of God, and the principle of creation, and moves through the fall of man and the course of history as God deals with fallen people. The first advent of the Messiah, the failure of his mission, the principle of restoration through indemnity, the meaning of Noah, Abraham, Moses and other Old Testament figures, and the significance of major events in world history to the present are discussed. Finally, *Divine Principle* presents the need for a second advent of the Messiah and argues that he has already arrived on the scene by being born in Korea.

It is interesting, however, that *Divine Principle* does not just start from scratch as a fresh revelation with no roots. Over and over it draws evidence from the Bible for the views that it espouses. But it does so by lifting only so much as will fit with the new revelation, the new Unification system of thought. That is, unlike a work of traditional Christian theology, *Divine Principle* does not start with Scripture and exegete the text, letting the meaning within the Bible govern the shape and form of the theology that emerges. Rather it proceeds in an orderly fashion to spin out its own system of thought using the Bible wherever it appears to fit. When the Bible does not easily square with Moon's thought, it is either ignored or distorted to appear to fit anyway.

This approach to Scripture is evident from the opening paragraphs of the main body of the book (Part I, Ch. i, Sec. I) which discusses the "duel characteristics of God." "How can we know the characteristics of God" since he is invisible? *Divine Principle* asks.[3] It then quotes Romans 1:20 which points out that creation reveals his deity. On this basis *Divine Principle* turns to creation to see what it is like. Immediately we are exposed to an extrabiblical set of notions. "A creation, whatever it may be, cannot come into being unless a reciprocal relationship between positivity and negativity has been achieved, not only within itself but also in relationship to other beings."[4] From this simple-sounding proposition the whole of *Divine Principle* might be said to derive, for from this point on, all of reality—God, mankind, the universe—is seen as a combination of the positive and the negative. "As for man, God created a man (male), Adam, in the beginning; then, seeing that it was not good that man should be alone (Gen. 2:18), He made a woman (female), Eve, as Adam's object, and for the first time God saw that His creation was 'very good.' (Gen.

1:31)"[5] Then immediately following this summary of the biblical text comes this commentary: "Just as a positive or negative ion, even after dissociation, is found to be the combination of a proton (positive) and an electron (negative), the stamen or the pistol of the plant and a male or female member of the animal kingdom can also exist only through a reciprocal relationship between their dual essentialities of positivity and negativity."[6]

The system which emerges in *Divine Principle* is based more on these initial concepts of positivity, negativity and reciprocity than on any idea found explicitly in any biblical text quoted. For example, the key concept of Unification theology—the "four position foundation"—which is central to the Unification Church's notion of salvation is based on these primal ideas of positive and negative. But one finds them nowhere in the Bible. Later one of their sources, the *Book of Changes (I Ching)*, is acknowledged.[7] We will see this below as we take up how *Divine Principle* understands the opening of John's Gospel. Here my point is to show that the Bible, despite the constant references to it, is really tangential to *Divine Principle*. All the intellectual framework comes from other sources—Eastern thought, modern science and Moon's own fertile imagination.

One further use of Scripture will be sufficient to round out my case. After explaining the "four position foundation," which is too complicated to elucidate here, *Divine Principle* says, "The whole universe will perform a spherical movement of unified purpose, centered on the four position foundation, when a perfected man and woman become husband and wife, with God at their center. However, the universe lost this center when man fell; consequently all of creation has been groaning in travail, waiting for the children of God—that is, men whose original nature of creation is restored—to appear and take their position as the macrocosm's center (Rom. 8:19-22)."[8] Here Romans 8:19-22 is called on to confirm the idea which ultimately unfolds in Unification thought that Sun Myung Moon and his wife are or are becoming the perfect husband and wife who will complete the process of salvation for the human race. This notion is, of course, found nowhere in Paul's letter. Occasionally, Moon's ideas parallel traditional Christianity and his use of Scripture is legitimate, but in his treatment of biblical characters such as Noah, Abraham, Moses, John the Baptist and Jesus, and their relation to his system, Moon simply ignores the obvious meanings of the biblical texts and substitutes his own.

This shift in the meaning of biblical texts is likewise clearly evident from the way in which the opening verses of the Gospel of John are interpreted by the Unification Church, the Jehovah's Witnesses and the Mormons.

John 1:1-4: Jesus, the *Logos* and the Cults

Among the key issues of life the concept of God is primary, for our concept of God tells us what we think of as absolute. When we ask ourselves, What is the really real? (that is, What is so real that nothing else could be realer? What has always been, always existed? What exists that has no other reason for its existence than itself?), the answer we give is our "God." Even if we choose, as the naturalists do, to say that matter (or matter and energy) alone exists on its own, we have made the material universe our court of last resort; the universe has become our God.

Christians, of course, are not naturalists, nor are cult members. So the question is, What kind of God does in fact exist? The closer a cult comes to traditional Christianity the more it is forced to wrestle with the biblical answer to that question. The Maharishi Mahesh Yogi may refer to the Bible upon occasion, but he is not required to deal with the Christian Scripture as if it had ultimate authority. The Unification Church, the Jehovah's Witnesses and the Church of Jesus Christ of the Latter-day Saints, however, accept the Bible as God's word or part of God's word. They, therefore, find it necessary to reinterpret certain Scriptures which traditionally have been thought to teach ideas these cults have rejected.

Among the texts that give these groups difficulty, one stands out as especially important—the first chapter of the Gospel of John, especially verses 1-4, 10, 14, 16-18. To see why this is so, let us examine this passage on its own:

In the beginning was the Word, and the Word was with God, and the Word was God. He was in the beginning with God; all things were made through him, and without him was not anything made that was made. In him was life, and the life was the light of men. (vv. 1-4)

He was in the world, and the world was made through him, yet the world knew him not. (v. 10)

And the Word became flesh and dwelt among us, full of grace and truth; we have beheld his glory, glory as of the only Son from the Father. (v. 14)

And from his fulness have we all received, grace upon grace. For the law was given through Moses; grace and truth came through Jesus Christ. No one has ever seen God; the only Son, who is in the bosom of the Father, he has made him known. (vv. 16-18)

These verses teach, so traditional Christian scholars say, that the God who has always existed has always existed with the Word [Gk. *Logos*], a term meaning not only *word* as expression, but *order, structure, rationality* and *meaning* itself.[9] That is, the Word is coeternal with God and is, in fact, deity ("the Word was God").

These verses also teach that this Word was and is personal. The *Logos* is not just an abstract principle of reason. Personal pronouns are used to refer to him, and, most importantly, he became flesh as "the only Son from the Father" (v. 14). The Gospel of John, in other words, sees Jesus as the divine Son of God, and as such just as much God as God the Father.

Third, these verses teach that the Word, the Son of God, was involved in the creation of all things ("without him was not anything made that was made," v. 3).

Finally, these verses teach that Jesus Christ uniquely displays the fullness of God's character. "We have beheld his glory, glory as of the only Son from the Father" (v. 14). Jesus is the great revealer of who God is (v. 18).

These opening verses to the Gospel of John set the theological framework for the entire book, and themes introduced here weave in and out of the fabric of the Gospel. In John 5:36-37 and 8:23 Jesus, for example, claims to be from God. In John 5:18 he "called God his own Father, making himself equal with God." In John 8:58 he claimed to exist even before Abraham. In John 10:30, he said, "I and the Father are one," and later in the same chapter, "the Father is in me and I am in the Father" (v. 38). Finally in John 20:28, Thomas comes to believe that Jesus has been raised from the dead, and Jesus accepts his worship, as Thomas says to him, "My Lord and my God!" All of these texts and many others in the Gospel of John confirm that the traditional Christian understanding of the opening of John's Gospel is correct. That is, Jesus Christ is indeed God, distinguishable from the Father but coequal with him and one with him.

Thus these verses have been central to the Christian doctrine of the Trinity. The deity of the Holy Spirit is not taught in these verses; that comes from elsewhere in John and other New Testament texts. But here, clearly, is key evidence for the Second Person of the Trinity. As we have seen above, however, it is just this notion of Jesus as God which so many of the near-Christian cults reject. They find it necessary, therefore, to give alternate explanations for these texts. We will look now at the various ways three of these cults try to fit these verses (or at least some of them) into their system.

Case 1. The Unification Church teaches that "Jesus, as a man having fulfilled the purpose of creation, is one body with God. So, in light of his deity he may well be called God. Nevertheless, he can by no means be called God Himself."[10] Any person, Moon teaches, can have the same deity as Christ.[11]

In fact, Jesus failed in his mission to bring mankind salvation, for he was unable to marry and found the first perfect family around whom could be gathered God's people in a perfected four position foundation relationship.[12] But John the Baptist had failed to convince the Jews that Jesus was the Messiah, and so Jesus could not fulfill his mission.[13] Rather Jesus' "body was invaded by Satan" and he chose to die on the cross and thus accomplish the "spiritual" salvation of mankind.[14] But full salvation requires "physical" salvation as well. And so that leaves the need for another advent of the Messiah who can with his wife fulfill the four position foundation, become the center of a new society of God's children, and thus provide "physical" salvation.

In such a theological system Jesus cannot be the "only Son from the Father" (Jn. 1:14); he failed in his mission and thus cannot be coequal with God. So how does Moon handle what appears to be the obvious teaching of John 1? The first time John 1 comes in for commentary in *Divine Principle* provides the answer:

Let us examine the fundamental theory of the *Book of Changes (I Ching)*, which is the center of Oriental philosophy, from the viewpoint of the principle of creation.

This book emphasizes that the foundation of the universe is Taeguk (ultimacy) and from this comes Yang and Yin (positivity and negativity). From Yang and Yin come the "O-haeing" (five elements: metal, wood, water, fire and soil). All things were created from O-haeing. Positivity and negativity together are called the "Tao." The "Tao" is defined as the "Way," or the "Word." That is, Taeguk produced the word (creative principle) and the word produced all things. Therefore, Taeguk is the first and ultimate cause of all existence and is the unified nucleus of both positivity and negativity.

By comparing this with the Bible (John 1:1-3), "The word was God . . . and all things were created through him," we can see that Taeguk, the subject which contains positivity and negativity, represents God, the subject who contains dual essentialities.[15]

The Gospel of John is not being seen here on its own within the framework of Hebrew and Greek thought out of which it arose. It is being easily and casually linked with Eastern thought. God is treated as parallel with Taeguk and the Word *(Logos)* as parallel with the Tao—a case of world-view confusion.

When John 1:1-3 comes up for comment again, the same principle of misreading is evident:

"Logos" is a Hellenic word meaning "word" or "law." It is written (John 1:1) that the Logos is in the objective position to God. In the meantime since God, as the subject of the Logos, contains dual essentialities within Himself, Logos, as His object, should also contain dual essentialities. If Logos were without dual essentialities, the things of creation, which were made through Logos (John 1:3), would not have dual essentialities either. Adam and Eve were the substantial objects of God, divided from the dual essentialities of Logos.[16]

Notice how easily *Divine Principle* states that John 1:1 says, "the Logos is in the objective position to God." But look again at John 1:1. No concept of objective or subjective is anywhere evident. These notions come from Eastern philosophy, *The Book of Changes*, perhaps, but not from John's Gospel.

Later in *Divine Principle* John 1:3 and 14 come up again for comment: "John 1:3 states that man was created by the Word. Consequently God's purpose of creation was that the first man should have accomplished the purpose of the Word by becoming the incarnation of the Word; but he fell without keeping the Word of God, thus leaving the purpose of the Word unaccomplished."[17] In traditional Christian theology only Jesus is seen as the Word incarnate, God incarnate. Adam and Eve were not *embodiments* of deity but were *creatures* fashioned "in the image of God" (Gen. 1:27). They were *created* beings, not part of God himself. But Moon applies the concept of incarnation to ideal humanity. Then, since Adam and Eve did not realize their divinity, *Divine Principle* goes on to say that "God attempted again to fulfill the purpose of the Word by re-creating fallen men according to the Word."[18] John 1:14 is quoted as proof.

This explanation helps us understand how *Divine Principle* is then able to see Jesus as Creator of the world without also accepting his coequality with God.

It is written (John 1:14) that Jesus is the Word made flesh. This means that Jesus is the substantiation of the Word; that is, the incarnation of the Word. Then it is written (John 1:3) that all things were made through the Word, and again (John 1:10), that the world was made through Jesus; naturally, Jesus may well be called the Creator. According to the principle of creation, the world is the substantial development of the character and form of a man of perfected individuality. So, a man who has fulfilled the purpose of creation is the substantial encapsulation of the entire cosmos, and the center of harmony in the whole creation. In that sense, it may be said that the world was created by a man of perfection.[19]

This rather difficult passage says in simpler words that Jesus is the Word because he expressed fully what a perfected human being is. And a perfected human being is really a microcosm of the universe. He contains in himself the essence of the whole creation. So *Divine Principle* concludes, "Seen from this perspective, we can understand that the Bible (John 1:10) only clarifies the fact that Jesus was a man who had perfected the purpose of creation, and does not signify that he was the Creator Himself."[20]

The straightforward language of John 1:1-3 ("the Word was God" and "all things were made through him") is thus set aside. The verses are lifted from their literary and cultural context, associated with the Oriental philosophy and molded to fit into a system of thought totally at odds with the New Testament.

Case 2. We have already examined the Jehovah's Witnesses attack on the Trinity (pp. 80-82) and their technique of translating Scripture to fit the needs of their theological system (pp. 34-36). Here we will look at how the New World Translation treats John 1:1.

The Witnesses, we will recall, believe that Jesus was not the Second Person of the Trinity but rather the first being created by God.[21] Bruce Metzger succinctly summarizes their doctrine of Christ: "According to Jehovah's Witnesses, Christ before his earthly life was a spirit-creature named Michael, the first of God's creation, through whom God made the other created things. As a consequence of his birth on earth which was not an incarnation, Jesus became a perfect human being, the equal to Adam prior to the Fall. In his death Jesus' human nature, being sacrificial was annihilated. As a reward for his sacrificial obedience God gave him a divine, spirit nature."[22] The Witnesses hold that Jesus Christ was neither coeternal with God nor coequal with God. And that means that John 1:1 and 14 cannot be interpreted in the traditionally Christian fashion.

The Witnesses solve this problem by retranslating the verse as follows (the words in brackets, says a note in the "foreword" are "inserted to complete or clarify the sense in the English text"): "In [the] beginning the Word was, and the Word was with God, and the Word was a god" (NWT, 1961).[23] Thus, while *Word* is capitalized and thus suggests divinity, the Word is said to be not God himself but *a god,* a lesser being.

Is there any basis for this translation in the Greek text? A long note in an early edition of the NWT gives a technical explanation, but this has universally been rejected by Greek scholars and no other standard English translation has even come close to this rendering.[24] Moreover, Christian scholars have studied this verse with exceptional care and are convinced that the NWT has no foundation for its peculiar translation. As one might imagine, the issues raised by the question are quite technical. Those who wish to pursue further the subtleties of the argument may wish to turn to appendix two.

The point remains clear: John 1:1 in its normal rendering supports the system understood by traditional Christians. Therefore, the Jehovah's Witnesses retranslated it to fit their system.

Case 3. The Mormon doctrine of God is, as we have seen, quite different from that of traditional Christianity. God the Father, his Son Jesus Christ and the Holy Ghost "constitute the Holy Trinity," but they comprise "three physically separate and distinct individuals."[25] God the Father already had a glorified physical body before mankind was placed on earth; his Son acquired a physical body by being born of Mary; the Holy Spirit remains spirit. But all three "constitute the presiding council of the heavens."[26]

Interestingly, this teaching, though far from that of traditional Christianity, does not require the manipulation of the opening verses of John's Gospel. The Mormon theologian James Talmage, for example, quotes John 1:1-3 and 14, and comments, "The passage is simple, precise and unambiguous. . . . That the Word is Jesus Christ, who was with the Father in that beginning and who was Himself invested with the powers and rank of Godship, and that He came into the world and dwelt among men, are definitely affirmed."[27]

The reason Mormons have so few difficulties with these classic verses and with other affirmations of the deity of Christ is that on the surface their teaching squares with Scripture. Even when Talmage turns to John 8:58, he sounds like an evangelical theologian, explaining that Jesus' remark, "Before Abraham was, I am," is an explicit reference to the Old Testament divine name, Jehovah (or Yahweh). But—and here begins a crucial difference—rather than holding that this statement confirms the Son's equality with the Father as in the Christian doctrine of the Trinity, Talmage argues that Jesus was claiming to be Jehovah himself. In Talmage's words, "*Elohim* [another designation for God in the Old Testament], as understood and used in the restored Church of Jesus Christ, is the name-title of God the eternal Father, whose firstborn in the spirit is *Jehovah*—the Only Begotten in the flesh, Jesus Christ."[28] My purpose here is not to investigate how Talmage draws this eccentric teaching from Scripture but simply to show that while John 1:1-3 is taken at a face value we recognize, other passages often used by Christians to confirm this teaching are seen by Mormons in a very different light.

The story of the Mormon treatment of John 1:1-3 does not end here. Though with similar results, *Doctrine and*

Covenants 93 deals with this text in a different way. *Doctrine and Covenants* 93, a revelation of Jesus Christ given to Joseph Smith, takes up many themes presented by John 1, and it does so in language drawn from John's Gospel. This revelation, which claims to complete that of John, comes in the words of the Son: "And John saw and bore record of the fulness of my glory, and the fulness of John's record is hereafter to be revealed" (*Doctrine and Covenants* 93:6).

Passages relevant to our interests here are as follows:
And he bore record, saying: I saw his glory, that he was in the beginning, before the world was; Therefore, in the beginning the Word was, for he was the Word, even the message of salvation—The light and Redeemer of the world; the Spirit of truth, who came into the world, because the world was made by him, and in him was the life of men and the light of men. The worlds were made by him; men were made by him; all things were made by him, and through him, and of him. And I, John, bear record that I beheld his glory, as the glory of the Only Begotten of the Father, full of grace and truth, even the Spirit of truth, which came and dwelt in the flesh, and dwelt among us. (*Doctrine and Covenants* 93:7-11)
This passage is, of course, an amalgam of phrases from John's Gospel. The "teaching" they contain looks familiar and straightforward. Moreover, to many people it will "sound" so much like the Bible that their critical faculties will be by-passed.

So far nothing unique is being "revealed." Then in 93:13-14 comes, "And he received not of the fulness at first, but continued from grace to grace, until he received a fulness; and thus he was called the Son of God, because he received not of the fulness at the first." Suddenly the revelation turns to the doctrine of *eternal progression,* a distinctive Mormon notion not found in John or anywhere else in the Old or New Testaments. Harry Ropp explains that doctrine this way: "Mormons believe that God [the Father] used to be a man but was able to learn how to be a god, and all Mormon men are planning on becoming gods just as they say our heavenly Father did."[29]

In *Doctrine and Covenants* 93:13-14, Jesus is seen as growing in godhood. In 93:21 mankind in general is offered a place in that same progression toward deity: "For if you keep my commandments you will receive of his fulness and be glorified in me as I am in the Father; therefore, I say unto you, you shall receive grace for grace." The voice of revelation continues, "I was in the beginning with the Father, and am the Firstborn" (v. 21), adding, "Ye were also in the beginning with the Father" (v. 23). The Mormon doctrine of the premortal existence of the human soul is thus introduced. Each person has pre-existed as spirit child who eventually is born and, by struggling to keep God's commandments, becomes able to progress toward deity.

This may seem a strange combination of truth and fantasy. But such is the teaching which results from the esoteric tradition in which people, like Joseph Smith, are accepted as God's latter-day prophets. If the Bible is held to be an unreliable guide—inaccurately transmitted, unclear or incomplete—and if we accept the authority of a new prophet, we can expect such a mixture. Even John's Gospel is subject to a rewrite.[30]

The Key to Understanding World-View Confusion

Here, I think, is the key to understanding world-view confusion: Instead of yielding to the intentions of the Bible, the reader simply searches for elements that superficially seem to agree with his preconceived notion; after finding those elements, the reader extracts them from their context and places them in his own. Responsible readers, on the other hand, are humble readers. They give up their own ambition to find in Scripture what they want to find. They bow before the meaning system they are dealing with. They say to Scripture and God who stands behind it, "What do you mean? What are you saying? Teach me. If I understood you yesterday, confirm that to me today. If I misunderstood you yesterday, correct me today."

Though Bible reading is our main concern here, the same attitude should characterize our approach to any piece of writing, even the writing of the cults. For first we want to understand *what* is being said. Only after that can we decide to accept it or reject it as a view we ourselves want to hold and act on.[31]

Chapter 10
The Discipleship of the Word

I f you continue in my word," said Jesus to those who after a long struggle had finally begun to accept his teaching, "you are truly my disciples, and you will know the truth, and the truth will make you free" (Jn. 8:31-32). If there is a single key to being responsible readers of God's Word, this challenge by Jesus is it. Jesus would have us immerse ourselves in his revelation, continuing daily to seek his perspective on life, his approach to the human condition.

But continuing in Jesus' word means more than simply reading and rereading. It means obeying, as is clear from the context of the Gospel of John in which these words appear. Those to whom Jesus was talking, in fact, were not prepared to go on with the task. They did not like the implications. For, they argued, if Jesus' word was to free them, that meant they were now bound like slaves to something false. This they would not admit. So instead, they turned on Jesus, told him he had a demon and tried to stone him.

Continuing in Jesus' word is indeed costly. It costs us our pride, for we have to yield to Jesus' better judgment. It costs us our self-determination, because we must follow Jesus' word wherever it leads. It may cost us our reputation, because Jesus' word is neither the reigning popular philosophy nor the philosophy of being popular. It will, in short, cost us everything that binds us to our own fallen selves.

But—and what a contrast it is—in becoming his disciples we will be made free—free from error, free from false values, free to be fully as we were intended to be, fully human, fully God's creation, fashioned in his own image, fallen (to be sure) but redeemed, restored to reflect again the glory of his goodness, truth and love (2 Cor. 3:17-18). As we continue in God's Word, this is God's promise to us.

To make the realization of the promise more concrete, I want in this final chapter to look back over the course of the argument of the whole book and to offer a few practical suggestions about how to continue in Jesus' word, how to avoid the errors made by cult leaders and followers, how to read the Scripture, so grasping its teaching that our own world view, our system, becomes more and more the biblical world view, the biblical system. There are, I believe, two general guidelines that we can follow. The first involves an attitude; the second a method.

An Open Heart and Mind

The most important factor in reading the Scripture is an open heart and mind. That chief of reading bugaboos, world-view confusion, stems largely from a closed mind and hard heart.

Think about it. Why should anyone reading the Gospels think Jesus taught that each of us is essentially divine? This idea is contrary not only to individual texts but to the fabric that holds them together. The primal sin from Genesis to Revelation is, in fact, in thinking and acting otherwise. And yet readers of the Bible persist in co-opting Jesus and his teaching for themselves. Jesus is turned into an Avatar, a great magician, a political revolutionary, a teacher of Eastern pantheistic monism.

The only way this can happen is for a reader to come to Scripture with the idea that he or she already knows what it contains. But we are fallen human beings. We do not know the truth before God shares it with us. Therefore, we must humble ourselves before the Scripture and let it penetrate our minds. We must yield to its frame of reference, sacrifice our preconceptions on its altar and be ready to accept its teachings no matter how strange they may first appear to be.

The attitude I am encouraging here is not just for new readers of the Bible, not just for those caught up in one of the cults, not simply for the Eastern guru who raids Scripture for its rhetorical power. I am encouraging all readers including the most "traditionally Christian" to be willing to abandon their preconceptions—even those based on yesterday's reading of the Bible—when they read the Bible again today.

When we come to Scripture honestly asking God to teach us from it, the Bible has a way of breaking through our previous encrusted notions of what it says. Sometimes this breakthrough is a freshening of our perception, a thrilling sensation bringing us to appreciate anew God's great and good character. The psalms, for example, often do this for me. And when I have no other thought in mind but to read Scripture, I often turn to them in anticipation of just such a quickening of spirit.

But sometimes the Bible breaks the mold of thought we had previously believed it contained. Our system, our world view, our preconceptions, become not so much confirmed as shattered. In fact, unless this happens to us every once in a while, we may not be as open to God's Word as we think we are. For—this side of glory—"we see through a glass, darkly" (1 Cor. 13:12 KJV). There is much we do not know and, worse, there is much we do not know we do not know. So unless we are sometimes surprised by Scripture, we may not be listening to it.

Think of yourself for a moment. Are you prepared to take your view of Jesus to Scripture, lay it on the altar and allow God to slay it by the sword of his Word? To be sure, if you are a traditional Christian, the hero so far in this book, you will hold the doctrine of the Trinity. Are you open to the Scripture changing your mind? What about your view of the Fall, of sin, of salvation? Can you be open to the notion you could have been wrong about what the Scripture teaches?

And what about the Scripture's view of Scripture? Ah! There's a problem. Can you consider as one among many hypotheses your preconception about the Scripture as God's Word, and look to see what the Scripture teaches on that very subject? Are you willing to follow *wherever* the Scripture may lead? If not, then, how open are you to the Scripture's teaching?

It is just such radical descent to the roots that Jesus was calling for as he challenged his would-be disciples to "continue" in his word. To continue in Jesus' word, is to follow where it leads, to act on its demands, to respond to its direction, to obey its commands without wavering. Nothing short of this is sufficient. That we fail even at our best to live up to Jesus' call to total discipleship should be our constant consciousness. That we follow with as much will as we can muster must be our constant intent. That only by the grace of God and the indwelling of the Holy Spirit can success be ours must be our constant hope and praise and joy.

A Method of Approach

All the good intentions in the world will not make us good readers of Scripture if we ignore the principles of good reading. We have seen how violation of these principles has resulted in bizarre and eccentric doctrines, binding people to twisted notions of God and false systems of salvation. It is time to reverse the image and ask, How can we avoid these errors and see God's Word clearly?

A straightforward approach to this question reveals five basic principles.

1. Recognize the systematic nature of all claims to truth. If the chief problem in misreading is world-view confusion, the first step in avoiding it is to recognize why this is so. Every claim to truth involves far more than the claim itself. The simple proposition "water is wet," demands a definition of *water* and a concept of *wetness,* and each of these concepts is based on further concepts and so on and so on.

All claims to truth are systematic. The task of good readers and thinkers, therefore, is to grasp the major features of the various systems into which these claims to truth fit.[1]

Jesus' statement, "I and the Father are one" (Jn. 10:30), for example, fits into a system which distinguishes between the essential nature of God and of mankind, such that Jesus is claiming divinity for himself in distinction from his disciples. The Upanishads' recurring phrase, "Thou art that," on the other hand, fits into a system which explicitly denies the distinction between God and man. So "I and the Father are one" is not equivalent to "Thou art that." The seeming similarity masks a profound difference.

How can one know this, then? Only by reading and thinking more deeply and widely than we are used to doing—and only by being aware of the systematic issues themselves. In short, these issues include the answers to the following questions: (1) What is the really real? the nature of ultimate reality? (2) Who is a human being? (3) What happens to a person at death? (4) How is it possible to know anything at all? (5) What is the basis for morality? (6) What is the meaning of mankind's sojourn on earth?

These are tough but absolutely basic questions. And while they may appear to have an infinite number of possible answers, in practice they do not. The answer to one question will limit the answers possible to another question so that only a few major systems really emerge. I have written about these in *The Universe Next Door*, taking up in turn theism, deism, naturalism, nihilism, existentialism, Eastern pantheistic monism and the new consciousness. If, for example, one believes that an infinite-personal God is the really real, then one cannot be a naturalistic existentialist and define a human being as an autonomous creator of his own human nature, as Jean Paul Sartre would do. One's concept of God limits one's concept of humanity and vice versa.

All claims to truth limit the possibility of other claims to truth. That is what makes truth systematic. And knowing this is the first step to seeing Scripture in its own frame of reference.

2. Base all your serious study of Scripture on a good text—the original language or a careful translation—and be sure to quote it accurately. No translation of Scripture is without its problems. Some passages have been notoriously difficult to translate, let alone fully understand. But the vast bulk of the Scripture is relatively straightforward. If, as I am, you are a student of the English Bible only, I suggest you have at hand a few tools to guide you in the more complex textual issues.

First comes your selection of a basic Bible to study. I suggest the Revised Standard Version (RSV), the New International Version (NIV) or the New American Standard Bible (NASB). You should have several other translations on hand as well. The King James Version (KJV), the New English Bible (NEB), the Jerusalem Bible (JB), the Good News Bible (GNB) sometimes referred to as Today's English Version (TEV) and the modern translation by J. B. Phillips (PB) are also useful and can suggest alternate readings that bring out nuances not found in your basic translation.

Second, you should have at least a small library of basic helps to the Bible: a Bible dictionary such as *The New Bible Dictionary* (Eerdmans), a one-volume Bible commentary such as *The New Bible Commentary* (Eerdmans), a large concordance such as Strong's or Young's, and a Bible atlas unless your Bible dictionary contains a good one.[2] Learn by practice to use these tools and add to them as your interests grow and deepen. A set of commentaries such as the Tyndale New Testament Commentaries (Eerdmans) and the Tyndale Old Testament Commentaries (InterVarsity Press) is expensive but invaluable. These are written by top Bible scholars but designed to be read by lay people and do not demand a knowledge of the original language.

3. Consider the literary context of revelation. As you read the Bible, let each text tell you what sort of "literature" it is. That is, consider the nature of each whole book of the Bible before pronouncing on the meaning of any given text.

The psalms are ancient Hebrew "hymns." Paul's books are "letters," some written to a specific church, some to a group of churches. The book of Amos is the "prophecy" of an Old Testament prophet and analysis shows that it is not so much "predictive" in nature as "critical," declaring what God demands and calling the Hebrew people and surrounding nations to return to God, live righteously and establish justice. But none of this do you need to be told. If you simply let the Bible speak for itself, it will tell you itself much of its historical and literary background.

Being aware of context involves attention to (1) the narrow context (set of verses or chapter) in which a text fits, (2) the larger context of the whole book of which it is a part, and (3) the intellectual and cultural framework of the entire Bible seen as it unfolds from the early revelation to Moses in the Pentateuch to the closing of the New Testament age over a thousand years later. That means that good readers will spend their whole lives without exhausting the task of seeing each text in context. But as you study carefully, year by year, you will find yourself getting a better and fuller sense of these three types of context, and your scriptural understanding will deepen accordingly.

Being aware of the first two types of context will help you to avoid some of the misreadings we discussed above: *collapsing contexts* (Misreading No. 5), *overspecification* (Misreading No. 6), *the figurative fallacy* (Misreading No. 8) and *the problem of predictive prophecy* (Misreading No. 9). It will not, of course, keep you from all error, but it will greatly limit the extent and seriousness of any errors you may still make.

4. Gather as much evidence as you reasonably can before drawing a conclusion. We saw what happens when conclusions are reached on the basis of only a selection of the relevant texts (Misreading No. 11). Our task, therefore, is to compare Scripture with Scripture, bringing in all of the relevant material we can find and thinking hard about it before making our judgment.

When insufficient evidence is available on an issue we are interested in, we should simply withhold judgment. If the evidence looks ambiguous—as on issues like the relationship between predestination and free will—we should be cautious about adopting a rock-hard position. And in all matters where Scriptures are vague or silent, we should not pronounce that the Bible has the answer. Many matters in Scripture are not *obvious* at all (Misreading No. 15).

Humility is a virtue not always found among Bible readers. But it remains a cardinal virtue, nonetheless.

5. Consult your Christian friends, your pastor and the Christian community of scholars, but do not defer to teaching which claims to reveal the hidden meaning of Scripture. Luther, as we saw, refused to acquiesce to the pressure from his peers and his superiors in the church, and this set in motion a religious reformation of striking proportions. We should follow his lead in requiring of ourselves what Luther required—to be convinced in our own minds of each essential biblical truth we adopt.

Tradition does have an important place in proper interpretation of Scripture. The way in which people in the past as well as others today read and understand the Bible acts as both a source of insight into scriptural teaching and as a guard to keep us from strange and eccentric readings.

This is similar to the principle of "intersubjective confirmation" in science where a right idea can be seen by more than one researcher. Without such a guard, we as Bible readers may become victims of our own private, and thus esoteric interpretation. In such a case we do not need a guru to mislead us; we are misleading ourselves.

Most modern misreadings leave parallels in the past, and these misreadings have been corrected by scholars already. The history of the church and the history of theology provides us with a helpful perspective on our own task as good readers.

Further—and this is an important caution—the Bible does not give any of us any warrant for strictly personal interpretation. The apostle Peter wrote, "First of all you must understand this, that no prophecy of scripture is a matter of one's own interpretation, because no prophecy ever came by the impulse of man, but men moved by the Holy Spirit spoke from God" (2 Pet. 1:20-21). The Holy Spirit is the ultimate author of Scripture and he is the final authority on what it means. We look, therefore, not only to our private reason and conscience for a final judgment but to the Holy Spirit who dwells with us and in us and in all God's people.

We should constantly be sharing our study with others, telling them what God has been teaching us, receiving from them accounts of what God has been teaching them, challenging each other to think clearly, to consider all the relevant evidence and to practice what we are taught. Our pastors and Bible teachers have a special function to play for they have usually studied more than we have and can give us guidance, keep us from eccentric and unjustified conclusions and point us to special, more technical literature and scholarship.

In the final analysis, however, we must find ourselves with Luther making our commitment to God's truth as our conscience informed by study and reflection and led by the Holy Spirit requires. And like Luther, we must live out the consequences, acting on what we know and believe, continuing in Jesus' word and being truly his disciples.

Appendix I
A Brief Definition of Twenty Reading Errors

T he following list is designed to be a handy reference to the reading errors which have been defined and illustrated in detail in the foregoing pages. The page references following each of the definitions refer to the longer sections devoted to each reading error.

1. *Inaccurate Quotation:* A biblical text is referred to but is either not quoted in the way the text appears in any standard translation or is wrongly attributed. Example: the Maharishi Mahesh Yogi says, "Christ said, 'Be still and know that I am God.'" This text is found only in the psalms. (pp. 32-34)

2. *Twisted Translation:* The biblical text is retranslated, not in accordance with sound Greek scholarship, to fit the preconceived teachings of a cult. Example: the Jehovah's Witnesses translate John 1:1 as "In [the] beginning the Word

was, and the Word was with God, and the Word was a god."
(pp. 34-38)

3. *The Biblical Hook:* A text of Scripture is quoted primarily
as a device to grasp the attention of readers or listeners and
then followed by teaching which is so nonbiblical that it
would appear far more dubious to most people had it not
been preceded by a reference to Scripture. Example: Mormon missionaries quote James 1:5 which promises God's
wisdom to those who ask him and follow this by explaining
that when Joseph Smith did this he was given a revelation
from which he concluded that God the Father has a body.
(pp. 41-50)

4. *Ignoring the Immediate Context:* A text of Scripture is
quoted but removed from the surrounding verses which
form the immediate framework for its meaning. Example:
Alan Watts quotes the first half of John 5:39 ("You search
the Scriptures, because you think that in them you have eternal life"), claiming that Jesus was challenging his listeners'
overemphasis of the Old Testament, but the remainder of
the immediate context reads, "and it is they that bear witness
to me; yet you refuse to come to me that you may have life"
(vv. 39-40), which shows that Jesus was upholding the value
of the Old Testament as a testimony to himself. (pp. 52-58)

5. *Collapsing Contexts:* Two or more verses which have little
or nothing to do with each other are put together as if one
were a commentary on the other(s). Example: the Mormons associate Jeremiah 1:5 with John 1:2, 14 and thus
imply that both verses talk about the premortal existence
of all human beings; Jeremiah 1:5, however, speaks of
God's foreknowledge of Jeremiah (not his premortal existence) and John 1:2 refers to the pre-existence of God the
Son and not to human beings in general. (pp. 58-62)

6. *Overspecification:* A more detailed or specific conclusion than is legitimate is drawn from a biblical text. Example: the Mormon missionary manual quotes the parable of the virgins (Mt. 25:1-13) to document the concept that "mortality is a probationary period during which we prepare to meet God." But the parable of the virgins could—and most probably does—mean something far less specific, for example, that human beings should be prepared at any time to meet God or to witness the Second Coming of Christ. (pp. 62-64)

7. *Word Play:* A word or phrase from a biblical translation is examined and interpreted as if the revelation had been given in that language. Example: Mary Baker Eddy says the name Adam consists of two syllables, *A dam,* which means an obstruction, in which case Adam signifies "the obstacle which the serpent, sin, would impose between man and his Creator." (pp. 64-66)

8. *The Figurative Fallacy:* Either (1) mistaking literal language for figurative language or (2) mistaking figurative language for literal language. Example of (1): Mary Baker Eddy interprets *evening* as "mistiness of moral thought; weariness of mortal mind; obscured views; peace and rest." Example of (2): the Mormon theologian James Talmage interprets the prophecy that "thou shalt be brought down and speak out of the ground" to mean that God's Word would come to people from the Book of Mormon which was taken out of the ground at the hill of Cumorah. (pp. 66-70)

9. *Speculative Readings of Predictive Prophecy:* A predictive prophecy is too readily explained by the occurrence of specific events, despite the fact that equally committed biblical scholars consider the interpretation highly dubious. Example: the stick of Judah and the stick of Joseph in Ezekiel

37:15-23 are interpreted by the Mormons to mean the Bible and the Book of Mormon. (pp. 70-74)

10. *Saying but Not Citing:* A writer says that the Bible says such and such but does not cite the specific text (which often indicates that there may be no such text at all). Example: someone says, "The Bible says, 'God helps those who help themselves.' " Or Erich von Däniken says, "Without actually consulting Exodus, I seem to remember that the Ark was often surrounded by flashing sparks." (pp. 76-80)

11. *Selective Citing:* To substantiate a given argument, only a limited number of texts is quoted: the total teaching of Scripture on that subject would lead to a conclusion different from that of the writer. Example: the Jehovah's Witnesses critique the traditional Christian notion of the Trinity without considering the full set of texts which scholars use to substantiate the concept. (pp. 80-82)

12. *Inadequate Evidence:* A hasty generalization is drawn from too little evidence. Example: the Jehovah's Witnesses teach that blood transfusion is nonbiblical, but the biblical data which they cite fails either to speak directly to the issue or to adequately substantiate their teaching. (pp. 82-88)

13. *Confused Definition:* A biblical term is misunderstood in such a way that an essential biblical doctrine is distorted or rejected. Example: one of Edgar Cayce's followers confuses the Eastern doctrine of reincarnation with the biblical doctrine of being born again. (pp. 90-96)

14. *Ignoring Alternative Explanations:* A specific interpretation is given to a biblical text or set of texts which could well be, and often have been, interpreted in quite a different fashion, but these alternatives are not considered. Exam-

ple: Erich von Däniken asks why in Genesis 1:26 God
speaks in the plural ("us"), suggesting that this is an oblique
reference to God's being one of many astronauts and fail-
ing to consider alternative explanations that either God was
speaking as "heaven's king accompanied by His heavenly
hosts" or that the plural prefigures the doctrine of the
Trinity expressed more explicitly in the New Testament.
(pp. 96-99)

15. *The Obvious Fallacy:* Words like *obviously, undoubtedly,
certainly, all reasonable people hold that* and so forth are substituted for logical reasons. Example: Erich von Däniken
says, "Undoubtedly the Ark [of the Covenant] was electrically charged!" (pp. 99-100)

16. *Virtue by Association:* Either (1) a cult writer associates
his or her teaching with those of figures accepted as authoritative by traditional Christians; (2) cult writings are likened
to the Bible; or (3) cult literature imitates the form of Bible
writing such that it sounds like the Bible. Example of (1):
Rick Chapman lists twenty-one gurus, including Jesus, St.
Francis and St. Theresa, that "you can't go wrong with."
Example of (2): Juan Mascaro in his introduction to the
Upanishads cites the New Testament, the Gospels, Ecclesiastes and the Psalms, from which he quotes passages supposedly paralleling the Upanishads. Example of (3): the
Mormon *Doctrine and Covenants* 93 interweaves phrases
from the Gospel of John and maintains a superficial similarity to the Gospel such that it seems to be like the Bible.
(pp. 101-04)

17. *Esoteric Interpretation:* Under the assumption that the
Bible contains a hidden, esoteric, meaning which is open
only to those who are initiated into its secrets, the interpreter declares the significance of biblical passages without

giving much if any explanation for his or her interpretation. Example: Mary Baker Eddy gives the meaning of the first phrase in the Lord's Prayer, "Our Father which art in heaven," as "Our Father-Mother God, all harmonious." (pp. 107-15)

18. *Supplementing Biblical Authority:* New revelation from postbiblical prophets either replaces or is added to the Bible as authority. Example: the Mormons supplement the Bible with the Book of Mormon, the *Doctrine and Covenants* and the *Pearl of Great Price.* (pp. 115-18)

19. *Rejecting Biblical Authority:* Either the Bible as a whole or texts from the Bible are examined and rejected because they do not square with other authorities—such as reason and other revelation—do not appear to agree with them. Example: Archie Matson holds that the Bible contains contradictions and that Jesus himself rejected the authority of the Old Testament when he contrasted his own views with it in the Sermon on the Mount. (pp. 118-24)

20. *World-View Confusion:* Scriptural statements, stories, commands or symbols which have a particular meaning or set of meanings when taken within the intellectual and broadly cultural framework of the Bible itself are lifted out of that context, placed within the frame of reference of another system and thus given a meaning that markedly differs from their intended meaning. Example: the Maharishi Mahesh Yogi interprets "Be still, and know that I am God" as meaning that each person should meditate and come to the realization that he is essentially Godhood itself. (pp. 23-30 and 127-44)

Appendix II
John 1:1 and the New World Translation

John 1:1 is a key verse for those who hold that the Son of God is fully divine. All well-known and respected translations of John 1:1 substantiate the doctrine. Take, for example, the Revised Standard Version: "In the beginning was the Word, and the Word was with God, and the Word was God."

The Jehovah's Witnesses, therefore, make a valiant effort to show that these traditional translations are inaccurate. In *"Let God Be True,"*[1] for example, the verse is explained by reference to the *Emphatic Diaglott,* which, as Metzger points out, is "a curious edition of J. J. Griesbach's Greek text of the New Testament (1806) with a wooden interlinear translation."[2] It was published in 1864 by Benjamin Wilson but is not now nor ever has been accepted in the scholarly community. The *Diaglott* translates John 1:1 as follows: "In the beginning was the Logos, and the Logos was with GOD, and the Logos was God. This was in the beginning with GOD," noting the difference between GOD and God. Then *"Let God Be True"* points out that the *Diaglott's* interlinear translation makes the distinction "still more clear": "In the beginning was the Word, and the Word was with the God, a god was the Word. This was in the beginning with the God."

In its various forms the New World Translation follows

the lead of this interlinear version. The 1961 edition, for example, reads: "In [the] beginning the Word was with God, and the Word was a god."

The Witnesses' most important public defense of their translation comes in a long note appended to the 1951 revised edition of the *New World Translation of the Christian Greek Scripture*.[3] Their defense hinges on a point of Greek grammar which the traditional Christian scholarly community has not let go unchallenged. While there has been much scholarly ink spilt over this technical issue, it is not my intention to discuss the details. We can, however, catch the flavor of the controversy in Metzger's treatment.

The NWT translation, Metzger writes, "overlooks entirely an established rule of Greek grammar which necessitates the rendering, '. . . and the word was God.' " Metzger refers to the work of Dr. Ernest Cadman Colwell of the University of Chicago who writes, "A definite predicate nominative has the article when it follows the verb; it does not have the article when it precedes the verb."[4] Colwell later discusses John 1:1 explicitly, noting that these opening words look "much more like 'And the Word was God' than 'And the Word was divine' when viewed with reference to this rule. The absence of the article does *not* [italics Colwell's] make the predicate indefinite or qualitative when it precedes the verb; it is indefinite in this position only when the context demands it. The context makes no such demand in the Gospel of John, for this statement cannot be regarded as strange in the prologue of the Gospel which reaches its climax in the confession of Thomas ["My Lord and my God!" Jn. 20:38]."[5]

After citing Colwell Metzger continues:

In a lengthy Appendix in the Jehovah's Witnesses' translation, which was added to support the mistranslation of John 1:1, there are quoted thirty-five other passages in John where the predicate noun has the definite article in

Greek. These are intended to prove that the absence of the article in John 1:1 requires that . . . [theos] must be translated 'a god.' None of the thirty-five instances is parallel, however, for in every case the predicate noun stands *after* [italics Metzger's] the verb, and so, according to Colwell's rule, properly has the article. So far, therefore, from being evidence against the usual translation of John 1:1, these instances add confirmation to the full enunciation of the rule of the Greek definite article. Furthermore, the additional references quoted in the New World Translation from the Greek of the Septuagint translation of the Old Testament, in order to give further support to the erroneous rendering of the opening verse of John, are exactly in conformity with Colwell's rule, and therefore are added proof of the accuracy of the rule. The other passages adduced in the Appendix are, for one reason or another, not applicable to the question at issue. (Particularly inappropriate is the reference to Acts 28:6, for no one has ever maintained that the pagan natives of Malta regarded Paul as anything other than 'a god.')[6]

Other scholars have pointed out that the NWT is not consistent in the application of the rule by which they claim to translate "a god." It would mean they would need to translate Matthew 5:9 as follows: "Blessed are the peacemakers, for they shall be called sons of a god," not "sons of God" (as both the NWT and the *Emphatic Diaglott* have it).[7]

The NWT's long note on John 1:1 also misuses the scholarship of other translators and Greek experts. For an extended analysis of the misappropriation of the work of Julius R. Mantey see Michael Van Buskirk, *The Scholastic Dishonesty of the Watchtower,* in which correspondence between Van Buskirk, Mantey and the Watchtower Bible and Tract Society is reproduced.[8] Walter Martin's analysis in *Jehovah of the Watchtower* is also informative.[9]

NOTES

Preface
[1] I owe this account to David Fetcho of the Spiritual Counterfeits Project in Berkeley, California.

Chapter One: The Methodology of Misreading
[1] Archie Matson, *Afterlife: Reports from the Threshold of Death* (New York: Harper and Row, 1977). Originally published under the title *The Waiting World* (1975). The book I was editing has since been published as Phillip J. Swihart's *The Edge of Death* (Downers Grove: InterVarsity Press, 1978).
[2] Matson, p. 122.
[3] Ibid., p. 123.
[4] Ibid., p. 128.
[5] *What Has Religion Done for Mankind?* (Brooklyn: Watchtower Bible and Tract Society, 1951), p. 32. Also see *"Let God Be True"* (Brooklyn: Watchtower Bible and Tract Society, 1946), pp. 9, 18.
[6] Article 8 in the Mormon Articles of Faith reads, "We believe the Bible to be the word of God as far as it is translated correctly; we also believe the Book of Mormon to be the word of God." To these they add the *Doctrine and Covenants* and the *Pearl of Great Price*.
[7] *Divine Principle*, 5th ed. (New York: The Holy Spirit Association for the Unification of World Christianity, 1973), pp. 9, 51, 131-32; Mary Baker Eddy, *Science and Health with Key to the Scriptures* (Boston: Trustees under the Will of Mary Baker Eddy, 1934), pp. 110, 126, 497.
[8] *Meditations of Maharishi Mahesh Yogi* (New York: Bantam, 1968), pp. 14, 63, 77, 89, 124, 155, 178.
[9] J. D. Douglas, ed., *Let the Earth Hear His Voice* (Minneapolis: World Wide Publications, 1975), p. 3.
[10] I am deliberately not documenting this quote because it comes from a book on the cults which, except for tone, is excellent. I am also not

identifying the cult founder in order not to indulge in the same attitude as the author.

Chapter Two: World-View Confusion

[1]In a recent Gallup Poll conducted for *Christianity Today*, 40 per cent of the American general public indicated they hold the Bible as the primary basis for their religious beliefs. Moreover, "only 23 per cent of the American public categorically deny that the Bible is God's Word while 42 per cent accept it as inerrant. It might have been expected that almost no one would be willing to risk believing the Bible anymore after two generations of liberal attacks on Scripture, the removal of devotional Bible reading from our schools, the adulation of science at the expense of 'naive faith,' and the increasing secularization of our society. That is obviously not so; the Bible has withstood all this abuse and, no doubt, will continue to stand." See Walter A. Elwell, "Belief and the Bible: A Crisis of Authority?" *Christianity Today*, 21 Mar. 1980, p. 21. The Gallup Poll also reveals an appalling ignorance of the Bible among the American populace. This combination of a low degree of knowledge and a high degree of respect for Scripture paves the way for unscrupulous religious teachers to co-opt the Scripture for their own use, claiming scriptural authority for essentially unscriptural ideas.

[2]Based on the definition given in my book *The Universe Next Door* (Downers Grove: InterVarsity Press, 1976), p. 17. See also the discussion in my book *How to Read Slowly* (Downers Grove: InterVarsity Press, 1978), pp. 14-17.

[3]Alvin Toffler, *Future Shock* (New York: Bantam, 1971), p. 155.

[4]I owe this illustration to the suggestion of Dr. James Bjornstad of Northeastern Bible College.

[5]Robert Linssen, *Zen: The Art of Life* (New York: Pyramid, 1972), pp. 105-06.

[6]Linssen's understanding is paralleled by some who would claim to be orthodox and biblical in their theology. See Ranald Macaulay and Jerram Barrs's critique of this distorted view in *Being Human: The Nature of Spiritual Experience* (Downers Grove: InterVarsity Press, 1978), pp. 38-52, 117-36.

[7]Juan Mascaro, ed. *The Upanishads* (Harmondsworth: Penguin, 1965), p. 31.

[8]For a series of interesting misreadings of the Scripture from the standpoint of Buddhism, see Christmas Humphreys, *Buddhism*, 3rd ed. (Harmondsworth: Penguin, 1962). Regarding "I am the way, and the truth, and the life" (Jn. 14:6), see pp. 93, 132, 146; regarding "Be still, and know that I am God" (Ps. 46:10), see p. 18; regarding the essence of Christianity, see p. 25; regarding "Whatsoever a man soweth, that shall he also reap" (Gal. 6:7 KJV), see p. 100; re-

garding the story of the man born blind (Jn. 9), see p. 104.

Chapter Three: The Text of Scripture

[1]Jess Stearn, *Edgar Cayce: The Sleeping Prophet* (New York: Bantam, 1968), p. 246.

[2]Jeffrey Furst, *Edgar Cayce's Story of Jesus: Selections, Arrangements and Comments* (New York: Berkley Medallion, 1968), p. 18.

[3]In Matthew Jesus uses the words *heart, soul* and *mind;* in Mark he adds *strength* to the list. Cayce doesn't mention *mind,* and *body* is probably his substitute for *strength.* In any case no particular problem emerges from this slight inaccuracy.

[4]*Meditations of Maharishi Mahesh Yogi,* p. 178. The only scriptural source for his quotation is Psalm 46:10.

[5]*The New World Translation of the Holy Scriptures,* revised 1961 (Brooklyn: Watchtower Bible and Tract Society of New York, 1961), p. 6. *The New World Translation of the Christian Greek Scriptures,* revised May 1, 1951 (Brooklyn: Watchtower and Bible and Tract Society, 1951) does insert the word *other,* but not in brackets, noting that it has been translated "as at Luke 13:2, 4, and elsewhere."

[6]*What Has Religion Done for Mankind?* p. 32.

[7]*"Let God Be True,"* pp. 9-10.

[8]Bruce M. Metzger, "The Jehovah's Witnesses and Jesus Christ," *Theology Today,* 10 (April 1953), 70. Those wishing to study this cult will find this scholarly article of great help; the entire article appears on pages 65-85 of the journal.

[9]Ibid., p. 76.

[10]Ibid., pp. 74-80.

[11]James E. Talmage, *A Study of the Articles of Faith* (Salt Lake City: The Church of Jesus Christ of Latter-day Saints, 1977), pp. 3, 7.

[12]The Book of Mormon, 1 Nephi 13.

[13]*Teachings of the Prophet Joseph Smith,* ed. Robert J. Matthews (Salt Lake City: Deseret Book Company, 1977), pp. 9-10.

[14]F. F. Bruce, *The New Testament Documents: Are They Reliable?* 5th ed. (Downers Grove: InterVarsity Press, 1960); and K. A. Kitchen, *Ancient Orient and Old Testament* (Downers Grove: InterVarsity Press, 1966). Readers who are interested in a more technical discussion of the New Testament manuscripts may wish to consult Bruce M. Metzger, *The Text of the New Testament: Its Transmission, Corruption, and Restoration,* 2nd ed. (New York: Oxford University Press, 1968).

Chapter 4: Scripture as Rhetoric

[1]*The Uniform System for Teaching Families (USTF)* ([Salt Lake City]: Corporation of the President of the Church of Jesus Christ of Latter-day Saints, 1973), p. C—1.

[2]This and the quotations that follow are quoted in *USTF,* p. C—5-9.

The text itself is drawn from Joseph Smith 2:5-15 in the *Pearl of Great Price.*

3*USTF,* p. C—1.

4Ibid., pp. C—29; E—12-15.

5"The Latter-day Saints base their belief in the authenticity of the book [of Mormon] on the following proofs: 1. The general agreement of the Book of Mormon with the Bible in all related matters. 2. The fulfullment of ancient prophecies accomplished by the bringing forth of the Book of Mormon. 3. The strict agreement and consistency of the Book of Mormon with itself. 4. The evident truth of its continued prophecies. To these may be added certain external, or extra-scriptural evidences, amongst which are: 5. Corroborative testimony furnished by archaeology and ethnology" (Talmage, pp. 273-74). All of these "proofs" have been effectively challenged by non-Mormon scholars. See, for example, Hoekema (referred to above) and Harry Ropp, *The Mormon Papers* (Downers Grove: InterVarsity Press, 1977).

6*USTF,* p. C—31.

7It is interesting to note that, while referring to many passages from both the Old and New Testaments, Talmage in his chapter on "God and the Holy Trinity" does not refer to John 4:24. Nor does Joseph Fielding Smith (president of the Mormon church) do so in his three chapters on God in *Doctrines of Salvation* (Salt Lake City: Bookcraft, 1954), I, 1-55. J. F. Smith does note, however, a passage in the Prophet Joseph Smith's Lectures on Faith (lec. 5, para. 2) in which the Father is said to be a "personage of spirit" and the Son a "personage of tabernacle, made or fashioned like unto man." This would seem to be closer to orthodox Christian doctrine. But Joseph Fielding Smith, aware of this problem, comments: "The Father and the Son are personages of spirit and tabernacle. As here used these expressions are synonymous and interchangeable. . . . A resurrected body of flesh and bones is a spiritual body in scriptural terminology" (p. 6n.). Then J. F. Smith refers to 1 Corinthians 15:44-45 which describes the resurrected body as a "spiritual body." We might point out, however, that Paul in 1 Corinthians was referring to the resurrected bodies of God's people and not to the nature of God himself. The term "spiritual body" is not used in the Bible in relation to God the Father.

8I am quoting in this section from the King James Version since this is the translation Smith had available and is the only one recognized as authoritative by the Mormon church.

9What then, we ask, explains Smith's vision? First, Smith may not have had the vision he actually claims to have in the "official" version of his life. In one early account Smith dictated concerning his first vision, Smith only mentions seeing one person, not two. In another later account (dated 1835) Smith gave of his first vision he "nowhere mentions seeing the Father or the Son. Rather he relates that he saw many angels, one of whom forgave his sins and testified that Jesus is the Son of God" (Ropp, p. 30). See also Wesley P. Walters, *New Light on Mormon Origins* (Salt Lake City: Modern Microfilm Co., 1967) and Jerald and Sandra Tanner, *The First Vision Examined* (Salt Lake City: Modern Microfilm Co.). A photocopy of the two accounts differing from the official version may be found in the Spring 1969 edition of *Brigham Young University Studies*. So, did Joseph Smith have the vision as recorded in the official account? Or was it a "sheer invention to enhance his reputation with the faithful" (Ropp, p. 30)?

Second, Smith's vision could have been just a dream—an incredibly vivid dream—one he mistook for a revelation from God. In this case, Smith would simply be a basically honest man who was misled by his own fertile imagination.

Third, it is also possible that Joseph Smith is a false prophet, claiming something that he himself knows is not true. In a warning against false prophets, Paul talks of "deceitful workers, transforming themselves into the apostles of Christ" (2 Cor. 11:13 KJV).

Fourth, the origin of the vision could have been Satanic, for in the same passage Paul adds, "Satan himself is transformed [marginal reading: 'transformeth himself'] into an angel of light" (v. 14).

[10]"Wisdom," *The New Bible Dictionary* (Grand Rapids, Mich.: Eerdmans, 1962), p. 1333.

[11]Ibid., pp. 1333-34.

Chapter Five: Scripture as Literature

[1]*Meditations of Maharishi Mahesh Yogi*, p. 178.

[2]The King James Version does not use quotation marks for any words of dialog, nor do the original Greek and, in this case, Hebrew manuscripts of the Bible. But the RSV punctuation accurately renders the sense of the text.

[3]Stearn, p. 256.

[4]Alan Watts, *Beyond Theology* (New York: Vintage, 1973; original ed., 1964), p. 108.

[5]Ibid., pp. 108-09.

[6]*USTF*, p. D—3.

[7]Ropp, p. 55, lists premortal existence of the human spirit along with twelve other distinctive Mormon doctrines not contained in either the Bible or the Book of Mormon.

[8]Joseph Smith, *Journal of Discourses* (Liverpool: F. D. Richards, 1855, VI, 3-4, quoted by Ropp, p. 14.

[9]The missionary manual *(USTF)* gives no biblical references for this concept (see pp. C—31-33). Readers who wish to check out the way

Mormons treat the Scriptures on this topic may, however, examine
the use of Scripture in Talmage, pp. 39-51.

[10]Matson, p. 74.

[11]Eddy, pp. 502-03.

[12]The close proximity of *Adam* (Heb. *'adam*) which signifies "red" or
"ruddy" to *ground* (Heb. *'adamah*) in Genesis 2:7 and 3:19 form a
basis for at least part of the comment. Though *Strong's Exhaustive
Concordance* does not suggest the concept "nothing," it may be legitimate to take *dust* associated with "ground" as suggesting the concept
"of little value." See also the article on Adam in *The New Bible Dictionary*, p. 13.

[13]Eddy, p. 338.

[14]Ibid., p. 579.

[15]Ibid., p. 584.

[16]Ibid., p. 586.

[17]Ibid., p. 591.

[18]Ibid., p. 584.

[19]Ibid., p. 579.

[20]Orson Pratt, *Divine Authenticity of the Book of Mormon* (Utah ed., 1891),
pp. 293-94, quoted by Talmage, 278-79.

[21]Talmage, p. 278. Talmage goes on to use Isaiah 29:11-12 as a prediction that the Book of Mormon would be taken to Professor Charles
Anthon at Columbia College who would refuse to read it, and that
the book itself would be given to the "unlettered youth, Joseph
Smith." See also Talmage's comments on pp. 267-68. Professor
Anthon in a letter dated February 17, 1834, completely denies the
statements attributed to him by Joseph Smith which puts in doubt
the whole fulfillment of the prophecy, even as understood by the
Mormons (see Anthony Hoekema, in *Mormonism* [Grand Rapids,
Mich.: Eerdmans, 1972], p. 93).

[22]Talmage, p. 276.

[23]There is no archaeological or other evidence for the existence of any
of the peoples mentioned in the Book of Mormon, despite the pro-
test of some Mormon scholars to the contrary. See Ropp, pp. 47-54.

[24]John B. Taylor, *Ezekiel* (Downers Grove: InterVarsity Press, 1969),
pp. 238-39.

Chapter Six: Scripture as Evidence

[1]The Bible itself contains many references to the value of the mind
and the importance of careful thought. See, for example, John R. W.
Stott's treatment of this theme in *Your Mind Matters* (Downers Grove:
InterVarsity Press, 1972).

[2]Irwin Ginsburgh, Ph.D., *First Man. Then, Adam!* (New York: Pocket
Books, 1975), pp. 22-23.

[3]Ibid., p. 53.

[4]Ibid., p. 59.

[5]Ibid., p. 60.

[6]Ibid.

[7]Ibid., p. 72.

[8]Erich von Däniken, *Chariot of the Gods,* trans. Michael Heron (New York: Bantam, 1971), pp. 40-41.

[9]Humphreys, p. 88.

[10]Ibid. See also his attribution of this idea to the apostle Paul, as well, again, without documentation (p. 86).

[11]See my discussion of this topic—if you wish, of course—in *The Universe Next Door,* pp. 29-38 and 132-46.

[12]*The Truth That Leads to Eternal Life* (New York: Watchtower Bible and Tract Society of New York, 1968), p. 48.

[13]Anthony A. Hoekema, *Jehovah's Witnesses* (Grand Rapids, Mich.: Eerdmans, 1972), p. 30. The Witnesses later recognized that Christian theologians no longer use this verse (see *The Truth That Leads to Eternal Life,* p. 24n.).

[14]Ibid., p. 31.

[15]Hoekema, *Jehovah's Witnesses,* pp. 31, 129-31. Metzger, "The Jehovah's Witnesses," pp. 72-75.

[16]*"Let God Be True,"* pp. 85-86.

[17]These texts are suggested by Hoekema, *Jehovah's Witnesses,* p. 32, and Metzger, "The Jehovah's Witnesses," pp. 71-73, as examples. Others include Mt. 3:16-17; Eph. 4:4-6; 2 Thess. 2:13-15; Jude 20-21. For a basic, straightforward presentation of the biblical basis for the Trinity, see Robert Crossley, *The Trinity* (Downers Grove: InterVarsity Press, 1977); or the "Trinity": entry in *The New Bible Dictionary,* pp. 1298-1300. The Jehovah's Witnesses emphasize the biblical texts which show the functional subordination of God the Son to God the Father. But this functional subordination is part of the doctrine of the Trinity and is acknowledged by the church.

[18]Metzger, "The Jehovah's Witnesses," pp. 73-74.

[19]Ibid., p. 73.

[20]Von Däniken, pp. 34-35.

[21]Ibid., pp. 34-41.

[22]*The Truth That Leads to Eternal Life,* pp. 163-69. According to Havor Montague, "the first direct condemnation of blood transfusions in Watchtower publications" came in 1943, but it was limited to its connection with immunization which they were then also opposing. *(Jehovah's Witnesses and Blood Transfusion* [Santa Ana: Christian Apologetics: Research and Information Service, 1979]), p. 15. This teaching was further explained in *Watchtower* (July 1, 1945; and December 1, 1949); *Awake!* (October 22, 1948, January 8, 1949, and September 22, 1949). By the early 1950s it was set firmly in Jehovah's Witness teaching and practice.

[23]This text is quoted as it appears in *The Truth That Leads to Eternal Life*, p. 166; it follows the NWT in all major particulars.

[24]*The Truth That Leads to Eternal Life*, p. 166. Hoekema, *Jehovah's Witnesses*, p. 38n., argues that the blood that was prohibited was not human blood but animal blood and that the reason it was prohibited was itself stated in Leviticus 17:11, "namely that God had appointed the blood of animals as a means of making atonement, and that therefore such blood was not to be used as food."

[25]The Witnesses do not consider that "keeping free from blood" may have been required more to avoid scandalizing the Jewish Christians than to confirm the continuation of the dietary laws of the Old Testament into the Christian era. See, for example, Hoekema, *Jehovah's Witnesses*, p. 38n. It is interesting that a much longer presentation on God's attitude to blood and blood transfusions contains no argument whatsoever for equating blood transfusions and "eating" blood. In "The Sacredness of the Blood of Free Men," a chapter in *Life Everlasting in Freedom of the Sons of God* (Brooklyn: Watchtower Bible and Tract Society of New York, 1966), pages 321-34 discuss texts relating to the prohibition of eating blood; suddenly, with no justification, on page 335 blood transfusion is introduced as if it were the same thing.

[26]*The Truth That Leads to Eternal Life*, pp. 162-68.

[27]Ibid., pp. 168-69.

[28]Ibid., p. 169.

Chapter Seven: Reasoning from Scripture

[1]R. Alan Cole, *Exodus* (Downers Grove: InterVarsity Press, 1973), pp. 159-60.

[2]Furst, p. 26.

[3]Stearn, p. 250.

[4]Eddy, pp. 331-32.

[5]Ibid. p. 107. Though Eddy does not mention this in *Science and Health*, Eddy's theology has its roots in Hegel and the teaching of Phineas P. Quimby. See John Gerstner, *The Theology of the Major Sects* (Grand Rapids: Baker, 1960), pp. 70-71; and Walter R. Martin, *The Kingdom of the Cults*, rev. ed., (Minneapolis: Bethany Fellowship, 1968), pp. 111-14.

[6]*The Truth That Leads to Eternal Life*, p. 48.

[7]*"Let God Be True,"* p. 89.

[8]*The Truth That Leads to Eternal Life*, p. 8.

[9]Ibid.

[10]See W. J. Cameron, "Spirit," *The New Bible Dictionary*, pp. 1211-12.

[11]See Hoekema, *Jehovah's Witnesses*, pp. 26-29, for a further discussion of this issue. Other verses teaching the personhood of the Holy Spirit include: Gen. 1:2; 6:3. Is. 63:10. Lk. 1:35; 4:14; 12:12. Jn. 14:26; 16:7, 14. Acts 8:29; 20:38; 13:2; 15:28; 16:7. Rom. 8:11; 15:13.

1 Cor. 2:4, 10-11; 12:1. 2 Cor. 13:13. Eph. 1:14. 1 Pet. 1:2.
[12]Von Däniken, p. 34.
[13]Ibid.
[14]See, for example, Meredith Kline's comments in *The New Bible Commentary: Revised*, pp. 82-83; and Derek Kidner, *Genesis* (Downers Grove: InterVarsity Press, 1967), pp. 51-52.
[15]*USTF*, p. E—12.
[16]See, for example, Ropp's summary of these theories, pp. 30-36.
[17]James Boswell, *The Life of Samuel Johnson*, ed. Edmund Fuller (New York: Dell, 1960), p. 99.
[18]Von Däniken, p. 40.
[19]*The Truth That Leads to Eternal Life*, p. 8.
[20]Talmage, p. 276. See the comments on this passage on pages 68-70 above.
[21]Eddy, p. 109.
[22]Humphreys, p. 26.
[23]Rick Chapman, *How to Choose a Guru* (New York: Perennial Library, 1973), p. 5.
[24]*USTF*, pp. C—15, 17.
[25]Mascaro, pp. 7, 31, 34. Coleridge and Wordsworth are also quoted (pp. 26, 28).
[26]*Meditations of Maharishi Mahesh Yogi*, p. 63.
[27]*USTF*, p. I—9.

Chapter Eight: The Authority of the Bible
[1]Quoted by Ronald H. Bainton, *The Reformation of the Sixteenth Century* (Boston: Beacon, 1952), p. 61.
[2]One might wish to argue that esoteric interpretation is merely a cultic version of a method of scriptural interpretation that developed very early in the history of the church. I am referring to the *quadriga:* the notion that Scripture contains four levels of meaning that was especially popular during the medieval era. "Clement of Alexandria had already in the second century distinguished four possible meanings of a writing: the literal, moral, anagogical and mystical" (Katherine E. Gilbert and Helmut Kuhn, *A History of Esthetics* [Bloomington: Indiana University Press, 1954], p. 149). These same four, though in slightly different terms appear again in Dante's letter to Can Grande della Scala (c. 1318), in which Dante describes how *The Divine Comedy* is "polysemous," that is, has many meanings (ibid.).

Most important, however, is Thomas Aquinas's treatment of these four levels in his *Summa Theologica*. Here he distinguishes (1) the literal (that sense to which the words plainly point), (2) the allegorical (in which "things of the Old Law signify the things of the New Law"), (3) the moral (in which the actions of Christ signify what we should do) and (4) the anagogical (in which the thing signified relates to "eternal glory," our heavenly state) *(Summa Theologica,* I., q. 1, art. 10). But all three extended meanings—(2), (3) and (4)—"are founded on one—the literal." The literal sense is primary. In fact, "nothing necessary to faith is contained under the spiritual sense which is not elsewhere put forward by Scripture in its literal sense" (ibid.). If this limit were respected, it would forever put an end to much heresy and other eccentric doctrine based on the so-called spiritual meaning of Scripture. Where, for example, does the Scripture teach that God the Father is our "Father-Mother God" (see Eddy, p. 9)?

Not all scriptural exegetes—even in the traditional church—have heeded Aquinas's warning. In fact, the Reformers found allegorical interpretation so rife with excess that they insisted on an almost completely literal approach. (See E. Harris Harbison, *The Christian Scholar in the Age of the Reformation* [New York: Scribners, 1956], pp. 34-37, 58-62.) This approach has come to be called the grammatico-historical method: a text of Scripture means primarily what its normal sense is when the text is seen in its literary and historical context. The grammar, that is, the form of the statement, is as vital to the content as the literary and historical setting in which the text occurs.

[3]Eddy, p. 330.

[4]See H. P. Blavatsky, "The Esoteric Character of the Gospels," *Studies in Occultism* (Pasadena: The Theosophical University Press, n.d.), 133-84. The original appeared in Blavatsky's magazine *Lucifer* published between the years 1887-91.

[5]Christian scholars contend that Jesus was referring to the revelation that subsequently became the New Testament. See Matson, pp. 6, 124, for one occult view of Jesus' words.

[6]See Marc Edmund Jones, *Occult Philosophy* (Boulder: Shambhala Publications, 1977), pp. 56-59. We might also include the Kabalah, a "repository of Jewish occult knowledge" influential in the Middle Ages (see W. B. Crow, *A History of Witchcraft and Occultism* [London: The Aquarian Press, 1968], pp. 81-86). See, as well, Crow's description of the gnostic dimension of esotericism (pp. 87-99).

[7]Quoted in Jones, p. 100. The strange story of Madame Blavatsky can be read in Colin Wilson's interesting history of the occult, *The Occult* (New York: Vintage, 1973), pp. 329-38.

[8]Quoted from *Lectures on Ancient Philosophy* by Jones, p. 101.

[9]Jones, pp. 53-54.

[10]From a peak in 1899 of some 10,000 members of The Church of the New Jerusalem in the United States has steadily declined. Currently it exists in three divisions with a combined constituency of less than 3,000. See Arthur C. Piepkorn, *Profiles in Belief* (San Francisco: Har-

per and Row, 1978), II, 654-61.
[11]Immanuel Kant, *Dreams of a Ghost-seer Explained by Dreams of Metaphysics* (1766). Walter R. Martin details Swedenborg's notable contributions to science and philosophic thought in *The Kingdom of the Cults,* pp. 241-45. See also the careful study of Signe Toksvig, *Emanuel Swedenborg: Scientist and Mystic* (New Haven: Yale University Press, 1948).
[12]"I intend to examine physically and philosophically, the whole anatomy of the body," he wrote. "The end I propose to myself in the work is a knowledge of the soul." (Emanuel Swedenborg, *The Economy of Animal Kingdom* quoted in George Trobridge, *Swedenborg: Life and Teaching,* 4th ed. [New York: Swedenborg Foundation, 1955], p. 46).
[13]Trobridge, p. 83.
[14]From "the concluding paragraph of the Introduction to *Arcana Coelestia*" (1749) as quoted by Trobridge, pp. 83-84.
[15]George Trobridge, who has written the Swedenborg Foundation's authorized biography, says that the "key-note of all Swedenborg's theology" is "the exclusive Divinity of Jesus Christ" (Trobridge, p. 104). This is an unusual twist in cultic theology. Usually if the Trinity is denied, the Father is the only person seen as God. Here Jesus Christ alone is God. The "trinity" Swedenborg views as incorporated within Christ but, of course, not in its traditional formulation.
[16]*Apocalypse Revealed,* No. 959, quoted in Trobridge, p. 138.
[17]It should be noted that Swedenborg did not accept as authoritative the entire Old and New Testament canon. None of the New Testament epistles have an "internal sense," he said. And he particularly despised the writing of Paul (Martin, pp. 246, 251).
[18]Emanuel Swedenborg, *Heaven and Its Wonders and Hell,* No. 1 (1758) (New York: The Swedenborg Foundation, 1956), pp. 1-2.
[19]Ibid., p. 3.
[20]Robert H. Kirvan, "Introduction" to *The Church of the New Jerusalem* by Marguerite Beck Block (New York: Octagon Books, 1968), p. xviii.
[21]*Divine Principle,* the scripture of Sun Myung Moon's Unification Church, does suggest a test of its esoteric teachings. For example, "Spiritual communication" with departed saints can confirm Moon's eccentric teaching about John the Baptist: "Any Christian who, in spiritual communication, can see John the Baptist directly in the spirit world will be able to understand the authenticity of all these things" (*Divine Principle,* p. 163; see also p. 153). It is interesting that *Divine Principle* speaks favorably of Swedenborg, saying that he "disclosed many heavenly secrets, with his spiritual eyes opened. His announcement has long been ignored in the theological world; but quite recently, with the increase of man's communication with the

spirit world, its value is gradually being recognized" (p. 463). On p. 474 *Divine Principle* associates Swedenborg with George Fox and John Wesley—virtue by association!

[22]Eddy, p. 107, 109.

[23]Ibid., p. 110.

[24]Compare, for example, Eddy, pp. 502-57, with the first eight volumes of Swedenborg, *Arcana Coelestia,* which has been translated and published in English in a revised and edited form by the Swedenborg Foundation. Swedenborg's treatment of Genesis is summarized in Trobridge, pp. 139-46. Block, writing from a Swedenborgian standpoint notes the possible influence of Swedenborg on Eddy and then comments: "Not only is the absolute idealism of Mrs. Eddy's metaphysics completely opposed to the dualism of Swedenborg, for whom both the world of spirit and the world of matter are equally real, but her claims to divine inspiration are naturally repellent to a church which has its *own* divinely inspired founder" (Block, p. 169).

[25]Matson, p. 116.

[26]Ibid., p. 74. See also pp. 76, 102.

[27]Furst, p. 47.

[28]Ibid., p. 77. Crow says that the Gnostic Cerinthus, toward the end of the first century, "originated the heretical idea of Jesus, still held in certain theosophical circles, which distinguishes between Jesus and Christ" (p. 90).

[29]Ibid., pp. 27-28. Marc Jones summarizes a number of occult reinterpretations of Jesus, including one by Max Heinel who says Jesus was not a Jew and that God's promises in the Old Testament now belong to the "Arian races in whom reason is being evolved in perfection" (Jones, pp. 54-59).

[30]STF, C—19-22. Talmage, p. 7. See Floyd McElveen, *The Mormon Revelation of Convenience* (Minneapolis: Bethany Fellowship, 1978) for an analysis of the "living prophet" as authority.

[31]Ropp, pp. 55-56.

[32]Joseph Fielding Smith, *Doctrines of Salvation* (Salt Lake City: Bookcraft, 1956), p. 191.

[33]*Divine Principle,* p. 51.

[34]Ibid., p. 131.

[35]Ibid., p. 132. John 16:25 is quoted in support of this idea.

[36]Ibid., p. 16.

[37]Ibid.

[38]Quoted from *Master Speaks* by Ronald Enroth, *The Lure of the Cults* (Chappaqua: Christian Herald Books, 1979), p. 103.

[39]*Divine Principle,* p. 163.

[40]For a brief presentation of this argument for the authority of the Bible, see John R. W. Stott, *The Authority of the Bible* (Downers Grove: Inter-Varsity Press, 1974); for an extended treatment, see John W. Wen-

ham, *Christ and the Bible* (Downers Grove: InterVarsity Press, 1972).
[41]Ernest Renan, *The Life of Jesus* (New York: Modern Library, 1927),
p. 60. The first edition was published in French in 1863.
[42]Ibid., p. 81 and 81n.
[43]Matson, p. 123.
[44]Ibid.
[45]Ibid.
[46]A. W. Argyle, *The Gospel According to Matthew,* Cambridge Bible Commentary (Cambridge: University Press, 1963), p. 53. Argyle locates
in the Dead Sea Scrolls *(Manual of Discipline)* a command to "love
everyone whom God has elected and to hate everyone whom God
has rejected."

Chapter Nine: World-View Confusion
[1]J. Isamu Yamamoto, *The Puppet Master: An Inquiry into Sun Myung
Moon and the Unification Church* (Downers Grove: InterVarsity Press,
1977), p. 74.
[2]*Divine Principle,* p. 10.
[3]Ibid., p. 20.
[4]Ibid.
[5]Ibid., p. 21.
[6]Ibid.
[7]Ibid., p. 26.
[8]Ibid., p. 39. For a simplified explanation of the four position foundation, see Yamamoto, pp. 74-76.
[9]See, for example, Leon Morris, *The Gospel According to John* (Grand
Rapids: Eerdmans, 1971), pp. 115-26.
[10]*Divine Principle,* pp. 210-11.
[11]Ibid., p. 101. Moon quotes 1 Corinthians 3:16 and John 14:20 as proof.
[12]Ibid., pp. 216-17.
[13]Ibid., pp. 157-63.
[14]Ibid., p. 148.
[15]Ibid., pp. 26-27.
[16]Ibid., p. 215.
[17]Ibid., p. 115.
[18]Ibid.
[19]Ibid., p. 211.
[20]Ibid.
[21]*"Let God Be True,"* pp. 34-35; chap. 3, "What Say Ye Respecting the
Messiah," pp. 331-44, is an exposition of Jehovah's Witnesses Chris-
tology.
[22]Metzger, "The Jehovah's Witnesses," p. 70.
[23]*New World Translation of the Holy Scripture,* p. 6.
[24]In addition to the *Emphatic Diaglott* discussed in a footnote below, the
Witnesses do, however, refer to one precedent in *The New Testament,*

In an Improved Version, upon the Basis of Archbishop Newcome's Translation: With a Corrected Text, printed in London, 1808 (NWT [1951], p. 777).

[25]James Talmage, *Jesus the Christ* (Salt Lake City: Deseret Book Company, 1977), p. 32.

[26]Ibid., p. 32, 39.

[27]Ibid., p. 10; see also p. 33.

[28]Ibid., p. 38.

[29]Ropp, p. 15.

[30]In his *Inspired Version,* a retranslation of Scripture which we have already discussed (pp. 37-38), Joseph Smith translated John 1:1 as follows: "In the beginning was the gospel preached through the Son. And the gospel was the word, and the word was with the Son, and the Son was with God, and the Son was God." As the Tanners point out, this "rendition of this verse is not supported by any evidence" (Tanner, p. 390). Even Mormon scholars can find no manuscript justification (ibid.).

[31]It is refreshing to see writers who are sympathetic to non-Christian ideas understand the difference between their own concepts and those of Christianity. Robert Linssen, for example, writes in his book on Zen, "The notions of sin, of original sin, of salvation and of remission of sin are foreign to Buddhism, according to which each human being is alone responsible for his misery and his joy" (Linssen, p. 74).

Chapter Ten: The Discipleship of the Word

[1]I have taken up this topic in much more detail in *The Universe Next Door* and *How to Read Slowly.*

[2]See R. C. Sproul, *Knowing Scripture* (Downers Grove: InterVarsity Press, 1977), pp. 112-25, for a much more extensive guide to "practical tools for Bible study."

Appendix II: John 1:1 and the New World Translation

[1]*"Let God Be True,"* pp. 35-36.

[2]Metzger, "The Jehovah's Witnesses," p. 67n.

[3]*New World Translation of the Christian Greek Scripture,* rev. ed. (1951), pp. 773-77.

[4]E. C. Colwell, "A Definite Rule for the Use of the Article in the Greek New Testament," *Journal of Biblical Literature,* 52 (1933), 13.

[5]Ibid., p. 21.

[6]Metzger, op. cit., pp. 75-76.

[7]Walter Martin and Norman Klann, *Jehovah of the Watchtower,* rev. ed. (Chicago: Moody, 1974), p. 49. See also Hoekema, pp. 128-31.

[8]Michael Van Buskirk, *The Scholastic Dishonesty of the Watchtower* (Santa Ana: CARIS, 1976), pp. 4-17.

[9]Martin, *Jehovah of the Watchtower,* pp. 48-52.

General Index

Scripture Index